W9-BLW-634

Contents

Overview

Lean in the office has finally arrived! We, the authors, have dedicated the last five years to creating, documenting, and improving the adaptation of lean practices into the administrative area—the office itself. Consider that 60 to 80 percent of all cost associated with meeting a customer demand—whether it be a part manufactured or a work request (i.e., an insurance claim, employee application, invoice, order, quote, or engineering drawing)—is an administrative function. The results—getting more work through in less time, and with greater ease—are nothing less than amazing and real!

There is no magic to it. *Value Stream Management for the Lean Office* will teach you the basic methods, combined with all the appropriate tools needed for you to get started in implementing your lean office.

What exactly does it mean to be lean? In 1990, James Womack and Daniel Roos coined the term "lean production" in their book *The Machine That Changed the World*. Since then, it has become common to use the word *lean* as shorthand for lean production. Lean production (or lean manufacturing) refers to a manufacturing paradigm based on the fundamental goal of the Toyota Production System—continuously minimizing waste to maximize flow. Being lean therefore implies a continuous effort to achieve a state characterized by minimal waste and maximal flow. To become lean requires you to change your mindset. You must learn to view waste through "fresh eyes," continuously increasing your awareness of what actually constitutes waste and working to eliminate it.

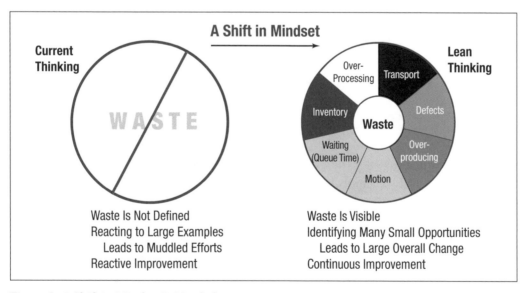

Figure 1. A Shift in Mindset Is Needed

Every organization recognizes that becoming lean is an important goal. However, many organizations are *doing* lean without necessarily *becoming* lean. Why? Because they try to "pick and choose" areas where they will be lean. Typically, such organizations sporadically implement improvements designed to minimize waste and promote flow without linking their efforts to a coherent, overarching strategy. One of the areas usually neglected is administrative work. This book shows you how to prepare your lean implementation strategy using the tools shown in Figure 2.

Some examples of administrative lean processes are: ensuring that customer orders are correctly entered to support overall strategic direction regarding on-time-delivery and DPPM's to the customer; ensuring that engineering development efforts align with strategic growth initiatives; and ensuring that new hires have global experience to help the company expand to new markets. The list goes on and on; the main point is to *utilize the lean tools to eliminate all variation within your existing office processes.*

Figure 2. The Lean Office Toolbox

Value Stream Management for the Lean Office is a how-to workbook that helps you immediately integrate these tools into your lean improvement efforts. We have taken the entire lean transformation process presented in *Value Stream Management* (by Don Tapping, Tom Luyster, and Tom Shuker), and in the video training program entitled *Value Stream Management: Eight Steps to Planning, Mapping, and Sustaining Lean Improvements* (by Don Tapping and Tom Fabrizio) that has worked so well on the factory floor, and have modified/adapted the process so that it works in the office as well.

Our successes to date are worth noting. Eaton Corporation's customer service department has improved order entry within eight hours from 62 to 98 percent by following this process and utilizing these tools. Engineering there has improved Engineering Project

Milestone Completion by 22 percent in each of the last three years. A small manufacturer, K&A Machining, Inc., saved $30K by not having to replace an employee that had left: after nearly two months of working with the lean tools during the process of interviewing candidates, the position was determined to be redundant.

The authors have many more examples, and the purpose of this book is to communicate the successful process. You will learn how to manage administrative value streams effectively using best practices from Fortune 500 manufacturing companies, as well as our own Premiere Manufacturing Case Study.

What Is the Purpose of This Book?

The purpose of this book is fourfold:

1. To simplify the fundamental lean concepts of demand, flow, and leveling as they relate to the administrative areas with the goal of creating a common understanding of these principles, which you will apply in implementing your lean office plan.
2. To demonstrate the overall lean *process* that will allow you to accelerate, coordinate, and most importantly, sustain your efforts and assure that everyone is on the same page. This process is called *value stream management*.
3. To apply this lean process to administrative work and show the changes that will result in the office.
4. To standardize lean office improvements with a structured, proven process.

Value stream management (VSM) is a process for planning and linking lean initiatives through systematic data capture and analysis. When you use the value stream management process as outlined in this book, your efforts to become lean will grow. This process was derived out of the study, research, and experience of the authors—not only from the successful manufacturing model, but also from some very lean offices. The manufacturing success model was tailored after Mercedes-Benz, Thedford Company, Wiremold, Inc., Pella Windows, and Eaton Corporation, to name a few. No book or workshop has conveyed the application of these tools in a simple, structured approach until now. Many books, workshops, videos, and the like only deal with topical issues, such as standard work, kanbans, or processes. What we provide is a structured framework for the ease of lean implementation as it has been successfully adapted to the office.

You will reduce costs as you eliminate wastes and promote the smooth flow of information and work.

Who Should Read This Book?

This book has been written for people with various degrees of lean understanding and experience. If you are just starting to learn about lean, this book will teach you an approach that will enhance your future implementation efforts. If you have attended some workshops or simulations, read some literature, or participated in lean improvement teams, this book can fundamentally change the way you approach becoming lean.

It is purposefully written for people at two levels who need to understand the concepts and the process (see Figure 3):

Top management must understand the process and believe in it before attempting to apply it within the organization. The VSM process provides this group with the necessary structure for commitment, as well as a communication tool that will satisfy their need for effective metrics and reporting.

Managers, supervisors, team leaders/coaches, and *co-workers* must fully understand how to use the process for planning and reporting, and also apply it in a way that makes it easier to get work off their desks!

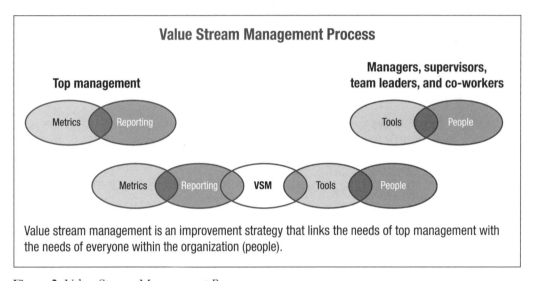

Figure 3. Value Stream Management Process

This dual perspective allows each group to gain additional insight into the other and, together, to leverage the power of the value stream management. The detailed case study used throughout the book demonstrates the usefulness of VSM to both groups.

Learning Features

As you implement VSM, it's important to ensure that everyone has a good understanding of lean concepts. To help you with this we have included the following learning features:

- **Guidelines and checklists.** Lists of questions and guidelines help you plan your lean future state and direct your implementation efforts.

- **Case study.** Learning to apply lean methods and tools is an adventure. You can and should study the tools and concepts, but the only way you will truly learn is by applying them. We have tried to show you how to apply the major tools and concepts by breaking down each of the eight steps of value stream management into smaller steps and including a case study based on an actual implementation.

- **CD-ROM.** Over 20 helpful forms and supplementary worksheets are included on the companion CD-ROM. The "CD" icon is used throughout the text to indicate when you can refer to the CD-ROM for additional forms.

- **Lean office assessment.** The CD-ROM includes a lean office assessment that helps you create a snapshot of your organization's current state and understand in a broad sense where you are now and what you need to accomplish to become lean. Performing the lean office assessment will help you isolate improvement opportunities and suggest metrics to help drive the lean transformation.

- **Glossary.** In the glossary you will find definitions of common lean terms and concepts used throughout the book.

- **References.** The list of references includes some excellent sources for further learning on the basic concepts and tools.

This book has the power to accelerate your lean learning and implementation efforts significantly. It will be an indispensable tool for study and reference as you make your way through the value stream management process.

Introduction

In the following chapters we will introduce you to the powerful tools of lean that were derived from the Toyota Production System. Throughout the United States and the world, we have spearheaded the adaptation of these tools in office/administrative environments, and in this book we share successful practices and lessons learned. We will:

- Introduce the lean concepts/tools/techniques as they relate to the office environment.
- Demonstrate the effectiveness of these tools/techniques through an actual case study.
- Reveal, through examples, the effectiveness of these lean techniques throughout a variety of office types.
- Show you how to apply the tools immediately so you can begin to adapt lean in your office today.

The overall goal of the tools and devices presented in this book is to eliminate non-value-added work or processes that serve no real purpose. We call this non-value-added work *waste*.

Let's get started!

The Value Stream

You could say that a value stream is like a flowing river that has no sharp bends, so the water runs smoothly. Whatever is downstream receives what flows from upstream with little effort. Each process in an organization can think of itself as part of the river as it passes its output to the next downstream internal customer. The process that is farthest downstream is the customer who buys the work units or services produced by the organization. In value stream management, we want to make sure that work units flow to customers as smoothly as possible. But this ideal situation rarely exists; there are usually sharp bends or restrictions in the process that impede a smooth flow. Lean utilizes the proper tools needed to make work flow downstream as smoothly as possible (see Figure 4).

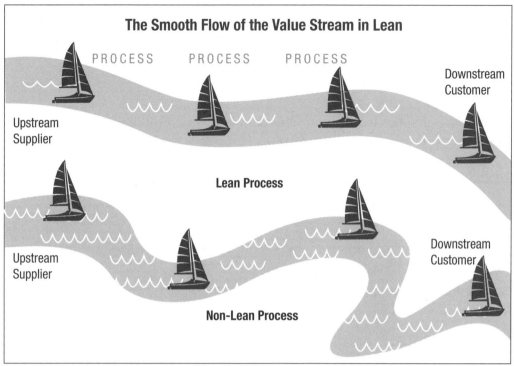

Figure 4. The Smooth Flow of the Value Stream in Lean

Work Unit

A work unit is a specific, measurable amount of work that can be customized and treated as a whole. You will learn how to group work units to ensure the most effective method to have them flow throughout the value stream without waste in the process. Some work unit examples are boxed below.

• **Customer orders**	• **Marketing reports**
• **Customer drawings**	• **Insurance claims**
• **Capital authorization requests**	• **Temporary employee requests**
• **Receivable invoices**	• **Payroll reports**
• **Payable invoices**	• **Blueprints**
• **International shipper forms**	• **Return material requests**

What Is the Value Stream Management Process?

We must first start with a methodology, so that whatever is done is done within a structured and proven process. Value stream management is just that: a process for planning and linking lean initiatives through systematic data capture and analysis. VSM consists of eight steps:

1. Commit to Lean.

2. Choose the Value Stream.

3. Learn About Lean.

4. Map the Current State.

5. Identify Lean Metrics.

6. Map the Future State (using the demand, flow, and leveling concepts).

7. Create Kaizen Plans.

8. Implement Kaizen Plans.

Value stream management is not just a *management* tool; it is a proven process for planning the improvements that will allow your company to become lean. The key ingredient in this "recipe" is the involvement of people throughout the process. You must involve the workforce, from the shopfloor to the office, otherwise your chances for success are severely limited. This process, along with a collection of practical worksheets, forms, templates, and checklists, will ensure your successful implementation of lean in the office.

> The flow of activities and work units that produce value for a customer is a *value stream*. When you apply lean management principles to a value stream, we call it *value stream management*. VSM will be explained more fully in Step 2 Choose the Value Stream.

The Value Stream Management Storyboard

The value stream management process employs the storyboard—a powerful tool.

> ### *Storyboard*
>
> A storyboard is a poster-sized framework for displaying all the key information for planning a lean implementation. It contains the goals and progress for each of the eight steps of value stream management.

 A small, blank version of the VSM storyboard appears on the inside front cover, with a completed version (from the case study) on the inside back cover. Your team will enter data and value stream maps on the storyboard to build a shared document of what you've done and plan to do.

For demonstration purposes, we will show the information being added to the storyboard during each of the eight steps. In practice, many teams find it easier to complete the storyboard during Step 7, to use as a management review document. Be flexible and use the storyboard in a manner that works most effectively for your team.

Visual management ensures that the organization's goals are clear and that all the information necessary to work as effectively as possible is easily accessible. Storyboards are commonly used at Toyota precisely for this reason—they help you see and understand the "big picture" and buy into the overall strategy.

 Although we recommend that you use the storyboard tool, we have also included an alternative communication format for reporting and planning your improvements, which is commonly used in many organizations. It is a "package" of forms that includes a team charter, meeting information forms, status reports, and a "sunset report" related to a value stream improvement process.

Why Value Stream Management?

Critical lean elements are often missing in current administrative areas. If you hope to create an authentic lean enterprise rather than a superficial one, you must learn the tools and methods of lean and how to integrate them. What is typically missing is a complete process that links strategic plans to daily work, while at the same time teaching the fundamentals. The eight steps of value stream management, followed sequentially, is that process. In addition, we have learned through experience that a successful lean initiative depends on four critical functions:

1. Make a true commitment to improving the value stream.

2. Understand customer demand thoroughly.

3. Depict the current-state value stream accurately.

4. Communicate, communicate, and communicate to *all* associates in the value stream!

Make a True Commitment to Improving the Value Stream

Is achieving a lean enterprise in which workflow is smoother and less costly, and people are less stressed, a "goal"? If so, then there must be the support within an organization to make resources available for this to occur. This, in particular, means that management must provide the necessary resources of training, benchmarking, time, and encouragement throughout the process. It all begins with a commitment from management. Not only does this book provide management with the necessary communication tools and reports required, but it also integrates the tool implementation in such a way that lean is learned, implemented, tested, and standardized, all while keeping everyone on the same page.

Understand Customer Requirements

Variation in customer requirements is not a reason for avoiding true lean implementation—only an excuse. It may take a little more work than expected, but you *can* understand your customers and incorporate them into your lean process. Analyzing the customer is a particularly important concern when you are choosing the target value stream (Step 2), mapping the current state (Step 4), and mapping the future state (Step 6). In VSM this sometimes means always knowing your "external" customer—the customer who finally pays for the product—but it also might mean knowing your "internal" customer—the next process in line in your organization.

Depict the Current-State Value Stream Accurately

Before you begin implementing lean, you must fully understand what you are currently doing in relation to cycle times, process communications, work standards, work capacity, and so on. Only by grasping the present conditions can you create a future condition and plan how to implement it.

In Step 4 you will learn how to map your current state accurately. Do not underestimate the importance of this part of the process. Even though you may want to jump straight to creating the future state, be careful about the assumptions you may be making. If you haven't depicted current conditions accurately, you will have significant problems later in implementation. Be accurate and precise! Do not rush in collecting this information.

You will notice the adaptation of symbols—called icons—in this map. We do recommend that organizations adapt a standard set of icons to ensure more effective communication. Please note, though, that it is the *process* that is important, and not so much the particular symbols you choose to utilize. The importance of team consensus and involvement, and applying lean tools with accurate visual representation, is the ultimate objective.

Communicate, Communicate, and Communicate to Value Stream Associates

Management professionals talk about and understand the importance of driving fear from the workplace and creating a "blame-free" environment. However, in practice, most organizations are far from perfect in this area. This is why it is particularly important to make the effort to treat everyone with dignity and respect. Good communication is essential to this effort. Telling people what you are doing and why—and expressing a sincere interest in making sure they understand—does much to create an environment befitting a lean enterprise. The more you communicate with people in this manner, the more you will earn their trust and gain their enthusiastic support.

We have already talked about the importance of visual management and visual communication in implementing lean. Remember that good face-to-face communication is equally important because it establishes the rapport that makes people receptive to actually using the visual tools.

Attributes of Value Stream Management

The value stream management process supports the transformation into a lean enterprise by providing a structure to ensure that the members of the lean implementation team are doing the right things.

Using the storyboard format, VSM encompasses the strengths of proven problem-solving methods:

- It provides a structured process to follow.
- Team recognition and ownership are included from beginning to end.
- Management review and reporting are incorporated.
- It provides a good form of visual communication.

- Changes and updates can be reflected as they occur.
- It provides for clear and concise communications between management and administrative area teams about lean expectations and about the actual work and information flow.
- Proven tools are used for implementation.

Any proven process can fail to achieve results if people do not apply it properly or if they lack a fundamental understanding of its nature. Following are some key points to remember about value stream management.

Value stream management is a process that:

- Links together people, lean tools, metrics, and reporting requirements to achieve a lean enterprise (see Figure 5).

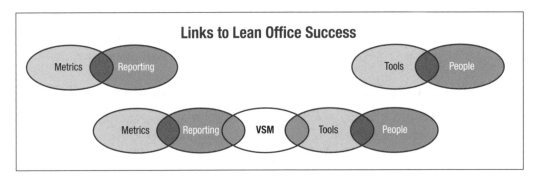

Figure 5. Links to Lean Office Success

- Allows everyone to understand and continuously improve his or her understanding of lean concepts.
- Generates an actual lean design and implementation plan.

Most importantly, value stream management is *not* a method for *telling* people how to do their jobs more effectively. It is a systematic approach that empowers people to *plan how and when they will implement* the improvements that make it easier to meet customer demand. It is not about making people work faster or harder; it is about establishing a system so that *work units and/or information* can flow through administrative processes at the pace of customer demand (see Figure 6).

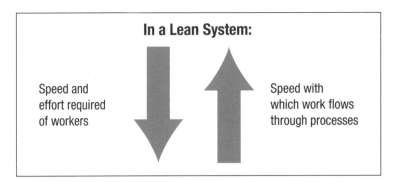

Figure 6. Meeting Customer Demand

Put People First

Value stream management not only ties together all the lean concepts logically and sequentially, it also involves *the employees doing the work* as an essential part of the process. Their efforts to eliminate waste are critical to successfully implementing and sustaining a lean system. Earlier, we talked about the importance of treating people with dignity and respect, and it is worth repeating. Never underestimate or disrespect people! If people and their well being are not a priority for the organization, then a true lean culture is not likely to evolve. People must be considered at all times. VSM will greatly assist in this, but in and of itself does not provide all the answers. It only works as well as management's ability to truly consider their employees' well being. Throughout each step we will focus not only on the physical aspects of lean implementation, but on the human issues as well.

To many people, lean implementation may look like just any other program. It is up to management to lead the commitment to lean and to demonstrate how and why it is different. The entire organization's commitment to lean will reflect the commitment of top management.

The world-class journey embraces people, tools, and support systems. We have found that simply applying tools such as value stream mapping, supermarkets, heijunka, u-shaped cells, and point kaizen workshops *in isolation* does not necessarily produce significant *sustained* changes in the workflow. It must be applied within a proven, structured process, with all the necessary forms and tools, in order to be successful.

As you read the explanations of the eight steps of VSM for the lean office, keep in mind the following lean management principles:

- Define value from your *customer's* perspective.
- Identify the value stream.
- Eliminate the seven deadly wastes.
- Make the work flow.
- Pull work, don't push it.
- Pursue to perfection.
- Continue to improve.

But even when you forget everything else, remember to work together!!

Step 1. Commit to Lean

Why Go Lean?

Why should employees want to participate in a lean transformation? That's simple—they have much to gain:

- Lean systems can make a business more competitive—and more likely to survive. A lean system can translate into greater market share. There is no guarantee of job security, but your chances are certainly better in a lean enterprise.

- There is potential for tremendous improvement in the office setting. While lean has gradually become an accepted part of production models, both in Japan and America, very little attention has been devoted to implementing lean in the administrative area.

- Lean seeks to eliminate waste, and employees function better in waste-free environments. Waste in the workplace causes fatigue, frustration, and burn-out.

- Lean systems encourage employees to become more actively involved with how the work is done. That involvement produces positive results. In a lean office, employees have a higher degree of job satisfaction.

- Events and activities that occur in a lean office are controlled by the workers—not the other way around.

World class is a never-ending journey, not a destination. A world-class organization is one that:

- Operates by the cost-reduction principle, which states that the only way to remain profitable is to not pass price increases on to the customer and to work on ways to save costs internally through the elimination of waste.

- Produces the highest quality in its business sector—zero defects.

- Meets quality, cost, and delivery requirements.

- Eliminates all waste (non-value-added work) from the customer's value stream.

You must stay the course with your value stream (or lean) initiatives. Lean is not a compromise: it is the *continual effort* throughout the journey that allows organizations to achieve world-class status.

Management Push or Worker Pull?

In creating change, we often talk about the difference between a *management push* system and a *worker pull* system. Management push—the typical change strategy in many organizations—involves management's issuing directives, or "pushing" improvement activities on reluctant employees. Worker pull, on the other hand, allows those attempting to improve the value stream to pull the resources and the training they need to accomplish their goals. Worker pull is the preferred method in companies aspiring to become lean (see Figure 7).

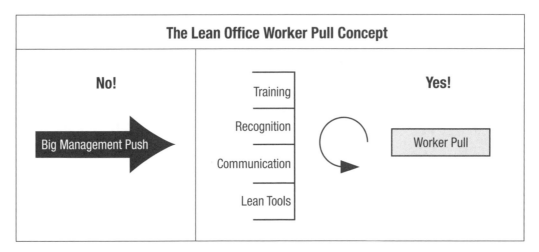

Figure 7. The Lean Office Worker Pull Concept

In a worker pull system, improvements and cost-reduction ideas (i.e., lean or waste-reduction initiatives) come "naturally" from the people who are most familiar with the processes, although it is management's prerogative to "nudge" people in the right direction. However, a natural worker pull system is unlikely to happen without proper guidance and support. Providing this is management's role. Many lean initiatives fail early on because management assigns a team to a project, assuming that this will demonstrate their commitment. But it is not nearly enough! Much attention, communication, planning, and buy-in are required for a project to succeed. It all begins with a process called *catchball*.

Catchball

Lean companies differ most radically from traditionally run companies in that information flows freely in many directions, especially from the top down and the bottom up. In fact, such information flow is instrumental to an authentic commitment to becoming lean. The beauty of this is that commitment grows stronger when information flows in both directions. Catchball makes this possible.

Catchball is simple. Regardless of who initiates a project (although it's most commonly a manager), that person articulates the purpose, objectives, and other ideas and concerns and then "throws" them to other stakeholders for feedback, support, and action (see Figure 8). In value stream management, the catchball process essentially begins as soon as a manager assembles a core implementation team and identifies an area to improve.

Based on the purpose, objectives, and concerns communicated by the manager, the team completes a team charter that defines the project in more detail and then throws it back to the manager. The catchball process continues until management approves the charter. Catchball is also used to reach agreement on the future-state map (Step 6) and create kaizen plans (Step 7).

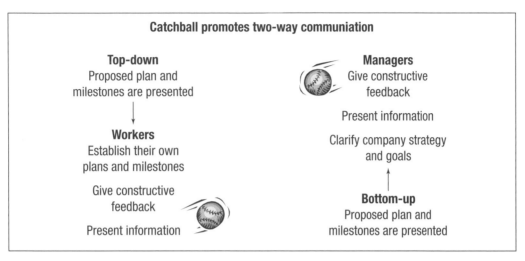

Figure 8. Lean Office Catchball

In summary, catchball accomplishes three things:

1. Ensures that management is committed to the core implementation team's ideas.

2. Ensures that everyone who should give input, does.

3. Establishes a credible and reliable structure for workers to initiate improvement.

Catchball is at the heart of a worker-pull system of improvement.

VSM in Action

A customer service office of five people shared a fax machine. They were frustrated about the amount of time spent walking to and from the machine to use it, wait in line, and wait for incoming orders. They often had to retrace their steps when that one fax machine jammed. And complete havoc occurred when the machine broke down.

Their proposal? Buy one machine for each customer service representative and locate it at his or her desk, at a cost of about $1,000 total. *Rejected by management*.

But when value stream management and worker pull (understood within the scope of the value stream process) kicked in, the proposal was accepted.

The savings? A minimum of 1,170 hours per year—enough to forego hiring a part-time clerical worker.

A Sense of Urgency

Worker pull and catchball are merely good ideas unless a third element is part of the mix. That element is a sense of urgency. If management doesn't demonstrate and build a sense of urgency, no one else will acquire it. Appointing a champion and a team leader who have a sense of urgency is the first thing managers must do. Taking action such as eliminating all temporary positions—which, too often, are used to plug holes rather than solve problems—is another way to convey the message that immediate improvements are needed.

Identify causes of problems. A sense of urgency to improve may arise when people begin to notice specific problems or inefficiencies indicated by:

- Time studies showing how and where time is wasted
- Customer surveys
- Cost/waste surveys
- Competitive analyses
- Benchmarking inside and outside the company

Key Management Activities

When we refer to "management," we are including vice presidents, directors, managers, supervisors, and team leaders. People in these roles make decisions every day that affect the flow of information and work units. They will become the "backbone" for lean implementation—the structure that supports the "living" value stream. Workers will become the "organs" for lean implementation, performing the vital functions that sustain and improve the system.

To reduce and eliminate waste effectively, employees must support the lean transformation effort completely. Ensuring employee support starts with communication between top management and all levels of the organization. Before beginning actual activities, as well as during them, top management must articulate the need to become lean. Management can do this by:

- Holding monthly, bimonthly, or quarterly meetings to inform people about new customer requirements, order status, customer complaints, increases in raw materials prices, new capital expenditure requirements, and so on.
- Demonstrating the pricing of current competitive products and sharing margins when possible.
- Displaying customer letters, both positive and negative, to all areas.
- Pointing out world-class examples; i.e., how L.L. Bean ships any product, any time within two days (but is continually trying to achieve it in one day).
- Assisting in the improvement process at some level, even if it is offering to help reorganize (or clean) an area on a Saturday or in the evening.

Once everyone understands the need, top management must find ways to open doors, allowing others in the organization to contribute to their full capacity (see Figure 9). This is accomplished through four main activities:

1. Identifying a value stream champion (or manager) and initial core team members.

2. Kicking off the value stream management project.

3. Going to the target area.

4. Reviewing all value stream improvement (*kaizen*) plans and returning to the target area throughout the scope of the project to help maintain momentum.

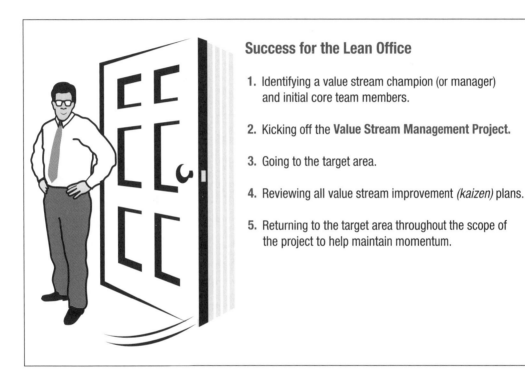

Success for the Lean Office

1. Identifying a value stream champion (or manager) and initial core team members.

2. Kicking off the **Value Stream Management Project.**

3. Going to the target area.

4. Reviewing all value stream improvement *(kaizen)* plans.

5. Returning to the target area throughout the scope of the project to help maintain momentum.

Figure 9. Success for the Lean Office

What Management Must Do!

1. Identify the value stream champion and the core implementation team members.

Top management's first task is to select a champion and make sure this person clearly understands the need for a lean transformation.

Value Stream Champion

The value stream champion should be someone with the authority and responsibility to allocate the organization's resources. Likely candidates include the sales manager, controller, business manager, customer service manager, engineering manager and office manager. In a smaller organization it may be the general manager or operations manager.

A value stream champion should possess the following attributes:

- A sense of project ownership
- Authority to make change happen across functions and departments
- Authority to commit resources

The champion will be responsible for reviewing the future-state map and reviewing improvement (*kaizen*) plans. He or she reports to top management (or the top person, depending on the size of the organization). The champion appoints the team leader, offers assistance to the team as needed—including outside consulting services if appropriate, training, reference materials, benchmarking, and the like—and acknowledges the team's work.

Once the selected team leader has bought into the project, he or she usually helps select core implementation team members and introduces them to the VSM process.

The champion also monitors the team's progress in applying the eight steps and is the embodiment of management's commitment and vision. The champion does not attend every meeting, but is available to remove any roadblocks to progress as they arise. Removing roadblocks includes the following:

- Assigning a cross-functional person to work with the team (this would be someone from another area who has no direct reporting requirements to the team leader).
- Allocating resources (i.e., training, benchmarking) that may have been suggested before but now are part of the value stream management process.
- Getting involved with personnel issues if reluctance is too great from a member on the team and the team leader has no authority over the individual.

Core Implementation Team

In addition to the champion, it's important to assemble a core implementation team for managing improvements. The core team will take ownership of the process and reach consensus on a team charter, following the direction of the champion. The team will create plans, communicate to all levels within the organization, make sure people are trained, and implement the value stream process. It's critical for team members to work well together, because every aspect of VSM requires a high degree of collaboration—especially mapping the current state and designing the future state.

Top management often assigns people to participate on the core implementation team. The team should consist of three to seven members. The core team is cross-functional; its members should be a good representation of the people who will be expected to sustain the system. Also, team members should be asked at the initial meeting, after the team charter has been created, what their role should be. The team should remain flexible throughout the VSM process in order to add/remove team members as needed.

You do not need to include someone from every area of the value stream; however, it's important to have team members who can communicate with all the areas that the value stream touches.

The core team should follow basic teaming guidelines:

- Identify team roles, such as leader, scribe, timekeeper, facilitator.
- Establish team norms.
- Include the value stream champion in the first meeting.

At the outset, the team leader should reinforce the commitment to lean principles and tools by explaining the difference between any existing system of quality improvement and the lean approach. The team leader performs several key functions, at meetings and in between:

- Supports team members throughout the process.
- Schedules meetings.
- Prepares the agenda.
- Uses the storyboard tool (or appropriate forms) to communicate the team's mission and progress to all participants in the value stream.
- Brings people with additional expertise into the team process as needed.
- Communicates with the champion and general manager on a regular basis.
- Understands team dynamics and the teaming stages and is alert for signs of resistance, which can be caused by inadequate knowledge of lean principles or unclear articulation of the need for lean transformation.
- Addresses nonparticipation early and privately.

Then you are ready to kick off the project.

2. Kick off the value stream management project.

The champion should attend the core team's first meeting to explain why the team was assembled and how team members were selected. He or she should articulate the need for applying lean principles and tools. This explanation should include the reasons for choosing the specified area of focus or value stream (i.e., competitive products on the market, customer demand for price reductions, customer demand for lead-time reductions, etc.). Finally, the champion should explain how the team and the project will support corporate strategy and goals. It's important to give the team as much clarification as possible—along with initial expectations—at the first meeting.

Make sure team members understand the overall objectives for their work together. Be sure they know that they can add and remove members as needed to reach their objectives. Other areas to address at the kickoff meeting include:

- A review of the lean principles and tools that will be used and what they mean to the team
- Expected duration of the project
- Expected communications
- Resources allocated to accomplish the objectives

- How to identify the initial value stream
- Questions from team members

It's important to document the team's formation and the scope of its work with a charter. A *team charter* is a document that lists the team members and their roles, and articulates the team's purpose, the expected duration of the project, resources available, range and boundaries of the project, and the mechanism for reviewing the team's work. The team charter should be updated to reflect changes as they occur (for example, the addition of team members or a change in the scope of the project or metrics).

Additional forms of communication, along with the team charter and storyboard, are the *Meeting Information Form*, *Project Status Report*, and *Sunset Report*.

The *Meeting Information Form* is used to convey the necessary items relative to running an effective meeting. It includes tracking action items, along with who has been assigned to each of them. It identifies team members and routes to other extended members of the team.

The *Project Status Report* is used to update the champion on a regular basis, showing the milestones progress or major accomplishments. It is also used to communicate to the champion if problems or issues arise that effect the timeline and, if so, what the team will be doing to get back on track.

The *Sunset Report* is a summation of the teams goals and accomplishments. It is used to brief others who may be attempting a similar project. It is used to capture what went smoothly, as well as what did not.

3. Go to the target area!

Most organizations are full of visible as well as invisible walls that separate functions or departments, making communication and teamwork difficult. Even in a completely "open" environment, with all the functions under one roof, the "walls" may still be there.

Breaking down these walls is one of top management's most important jobs. Before the walls can come down, however, managers must understand what is going on in their organization. The only way this can happen is by visiting the target area and observing firsthand what is going on there. It is more effective for management to go to the target area than for workers to come to the management area. Remember, the workers are busy creating value for your customers—fulfilling orders, answering customer questions, and so on. Management, supervisors, and team leaders must go to the work area and aggressively address employee concerns, as well as recognize the improvements workers are making to their areas.

If the champion is the VP of sales, then he or she would need to visit the sales department specifically to view its storyboard and comment on its progress to date. Rewarding and recognizing the improvements made is an important aspect of going to the work area.

4. Review all value stream improvement proposals.

After analyzing the current state and mapping a future state, the team presents lean improvement proposals, called *kaizen plans*, to management in Step 7. Management should review the team's ideas with great respect and care because the team has spent considerable time and effort, and has overcome many obstacles, to get where they are. During the review, management should:

- Thank the team for its hard work.
- Gain an understanding of the team's plan and rationale.
- Ensure consensus has been achieved and inquire whether everyone connected to the value stream is aware of the proposal.
- Offer additional resources to assist the team, if needed—this may involve outside consulting services, benchmarking trips to other organizations, and so on.
- Thank the team *again* for its hard work.

Reaffirm for team members how their work has supported corporate-level strategies and goals. Explain how their improvements are helping to strengthen the entire company—not forcing people out of jobs. Finally, focus on what you can do to make their jobs easier in improving the value stream.

5. Return to the target area throughout the scope of the project to maintain momentum.

How often have you heard about the "project *du jour*"—the project of the day? Most projects are not sustainable because the initial resources and attention devoted to them are quickly directed elsewhere. The result? Most workers are inclined to wait and see if management is truly committed. To show that commitment, managers must sustain an ongoing interest in the project and a visible presence in the target area. But this is more than just a management strategy. This is where the real story about the functioning of your value streams is being told.

Sustaining the Commitment to Lean

To ensure significant improvements in workflow, management must sustain the commitment to lean throughout the process. Even in cases where there are great expectations and projected cost savings, the project can get derailed. Once the impetus for a project is lost, it may never be resurrected.

There are a number of reasons why the process may fail. One of the main causes is management's failure to follow through with resource commitment. This may occur because the area of focus is not critical to the strategic direction of the company, because priorities change, or because no tools exist to ensure that the resources are being committed in the areas required. Other problems that may arise are:

- Failure to clearly communicate what is required from the start
- Lack of understanding of the area of focus
- Ineffective measurements
- Inability to see the *future state*
- Inability to focus on the value stream selected

Have You Heard These Comments?

"I don't know why, but our team has not met in two months. But here we are again."

"The proposals for improvements were submitted, but there has not been a response for over six weeks. I could be doing something of value. This was supposedly the 'hot' project six weeks ago."

"Our area needs to improve, but since we interface with the entire organization, it's just easier to continue the way we are doing things. This meeting is pointless."

"No one meets deadlines we are agreeing on. It is like all cross-functional teams—no wonder we are getting further and further behind."

"I have no idea why I am on this team."

"There is not enough time in the day to get everything done. But here I am, in another meeting."

Comments and questions like these can be eliminated once you understand and incorporate the value stream management process into your organization.

But VSM is not a cure-all. It is a proven process with a structured format that will allow you to dramatically increase your ability to improve and to sustain those improvements. The ultimate goal is to make your whole organization *faster*, *smarter*, and *leaner* than your competition.

Management Commitment Checklist

Management shows its commitment to lean by:

✓ Allocating the time and resources for training
✓ Providing clear incentives for the team's success
✓ Constantly communicating with the team and monitoring its activities
✓ Removing roadblocks that hinder the team's progress
✓ Establishing and maintaining clarity of purpose
✓ Allocating appropriate dollars within a short time period
✓ Staying flexible with the dates and times of the project
✓ Staying involved

You *do not* have commitment when management:

- Repeatedly postpones the kickoff meeting
- Does not attend, or somehow communicate to the team during, the kickoff meeting
- Does not allocate time for training or benchmarking
- Provides no additional rewards or incentives
- Does not respond to requests for expenditures within an expected time frame
- Shows little interest in what the team is doing

Lean implementation is simple in concept, challenging to implement, and even more challenging to sustain. It demands disciplined and passionate people to lead the charge. Transformation to a lean state does not occur randomly or naturally in organizations; it requires management commitment, detailed planning, committed people to lead the daily activities, involvement by everyone, and working knowledge of the tools.

Step 1: Commit to Lean
Conditions That Must Be Met

- A target project linked to a strategic plan
- Commitment of appropriate resources for success
- Willingness to provide time to the lean improvement initiative
- Demonstrated willingness to sustain effort over time
- Willingness to dedicate a person as project manager or champion

---

Keys to Successful Implementation

In order to successfully complete Step 1, management must adhere to the following guidelines.

1. Communicate, communicate, communicate.

Begin the value stream management process by initiating communication with all areas involved. If an operational or functional area is not represented on the implementation team, additional effort should be made to ensure communication with the people in that area. A storyboard (or its equivalent) should be posted in common areas and referred to in company newsletters and monthly meetings. Value stream management can deliver only if it is fully communicated to all levels of the organization.

2. Allow for experimentation.

Experimentation—without disruption to the system—is key. It is a mistake for a champion to insist on a rigid timeline for implementation and to dispense with beta testing. The successful implementation of administrative lean requires detailed planning, testing new tools for effectiveness, and adapting these tools to administrative areas while ensuring that the customer, whether internal or external, is not adversely affected.

3. Be flexible in applying tools.

While implementing lean, you must keep in mind the overall concept but adapt to your people, processes, and customer. Lean implementation means taking small incremental steps that will eventually attain the significant results expected.

PREMIERE CASE STUDY—STEP 1

Throughout the eight steps of the value stream management process, we will refer to a case study involving Premiere Manufacturing, Inc., to demonstrate how the process is implemented. Premiere is an actual company that applied the eight steps; we have changed the name and simplified some facts for clarity.

Background: The Present Situation

Premiere Manufacturing, Inc., is a Tier 1 supplier to the automotive industry. Premiere has received numerous awards for quality, cost, and delivery over the years. Their mission statement and strategic focus are set out in Figure 10.

Mission Statement

Premiere Manufacturing, Inc. will consistently exceed customer expectations in quality, cost, delivery, and customer service. This will be accomplished through a culture that understands and applies lean techniques.

Figure 10. Premiere's Mission Statement and Strategic Focus

Premiere's latest customer survey indicates a two-year negative trend in customer satisfaction, specifically as regards the responsiveness of the customer service department in handling orders, which has taken a drastic downturn the past year from the average. The results of the customer survey are shown in Figure 11.

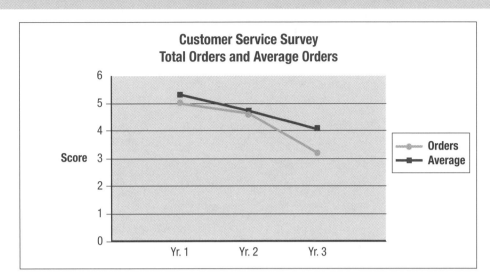

Figure 11. Premiere Case Study Customer Service Survey

The customer service department has been recording the following metrics for the past six months with the following results:

- Order entry on-time delivery (OTD) (within eight hours), 32%
- Returned work units response (within eight hours), 58%
- Errors as defective parts per million (DPPM)—internal > 2,500

Each year problem-solving teams were formed to address customer issues, but little or no improvement occurred between successive years. Something had to change. Management realized that the customer service department is the daily front line to the customer, and wanted to understand why the trend was negative. The most obvious explanation was that business had increased by 30 percent cumulatively over the past two years, with no increase in workers.

After instituting value stream management processes, Premiere's manufacturing operation had recently attained 99+ percent OTD within a two-year span, which they attributed mainly to their commitment to lean. In addition, quality has improved to <100 defects per million (DPPM) and costs decreased by an average of 6 percent per year.

Team Formation and Kickoff Meeting

The general manager proposes that the customer service department staff learn all they can about lean and how to apply lean principles in their area. Following this proposal, the sales manager assembles a team that consists of the following members:

- Sales manager: value stream champion
- Customer service manager: team leader
- Three customer service representatives: team members
- Two mailroom representatives: extended team members

The sales manager explains to the team that applying lean practices will produce the desired improvement in customer satisfaction and also covers the following points during the kickoff meeting:

- He explains the value stream management process and its importance, and outlines the time frame for the team's activities.
- He explains how team members were chosen and tells them that each member is critical to making the changes needed in customer service.
- He expresses keen interest in reviewing their process improvement (or kaizen) plans, once they have completed them.
- He solicits questions and asks the team what he can do as champion to support its efforts.

The sales manager promises to monitor the team's progress and visit the customer service area frequently to address team members' concerns. He discusses his expectations regarding how the team will report on its activities (i.e., the charter, meeting information form, and status reports), and gives an overview of how the team will select the value stream to focus on in Step 2.

At the initial meeting the team will discuss the VSM process and continue on to Step 2. They will also discuss roadblocks, team rules, meeting times, and so on to ensure appropriate communication. As the storyboard is introduced, the team will determine who will be responsible for creating the visual display and where it will be posted.

The team's first action after the kickoff meeting is to create a team charter that incorporates all the relevant information communicated.

Premiere Manufacturing, Inc. Team Charter

Mission—Charter:
- The customer service kaizen team was formed to improve customer service standards. This was in response to falling customer safisfaction scores in the past 2 years.

Deliverables:
- A more professional approach to dealing with customers.
- Improved response time to returns.
- Improved response times to expediting of orders.
- Improved internal communications.
- Improved response time to processing orders.
- Improved on-time delivery performance.

Expected Scope/Approach/Activities:
- Form a kaizen team.
- Process map all activities.
- Identify problem areas and root causes.
- Adopt kaizen tools.
- Measure all key activities to improve.
- Create current- and future-state value stream maps.
- Create implementation plans.

Strategic Alignment Factors:
Premiere's goals—
- Growth
- Total business excellence
- Critical success factors

Timeframe/Duration:
- Start date – 6/3
- End date – 12/30
- Duration – 30 weeks

Team Resources:

Role	Name(s)	Participation Level	Skills Required
Team champion	R.W.	P/Time	•
Core team members	L.D.	Full	•
	D.W.	Full	•
	J.M.	Full	•
	S.L	Full	•
Extended team members	M.B.	As needed	•
	M.D.	As needed	•

Team Process:

Process Item	Frequency	Audience/Distribution,
Information distribution	After meetings	Team members, team champion
Team meetings	Weekly then monthly	
Status reporting	Weekly then monthly	
LAN storage location for team documents:		J: CSR/VSM

Premiere Manufacturing, Inc. Team Charter, continued

Expected Results:

Benefits (What results will be gained?)	Metrics (How will the results be measured?)
1. A more professional approach to dealing with customers.	1. Local customer survey results.
2. Improved response time to returns.	2. QOS measure.
3. Improved response time to expediting of orders.	3. Local customer survey results.
4. Improved internal communications.	4. Local customer survey results.
5. Improved response time to processing orders.	5. QOS measure.
6. Improved on-time delivery performance.	6. Top level QOS.

Key Customers and Suppliers:

Company Name (Ext.) or Functional Area (Int.)	Relationship		Level			Reviewer(s) Names
	Customer	Supplier	Economic	Operational	User/Tech	
External						
Key Customers	x					
Internal						
Engineering		x				
Information Tech.						
Manufacturing	x					
Marketing		x				
Purchasing		x				
Quality		x				
Planning		x				

Assumptions:

- Employment levels remain the same
- Time allocated to VSM process
- Customer survey improves

Risks:

- Business downturn
- Customer survey does not improve

Internal Issues:

- Champion allocates resources
- Meetings are effective
- True teaming occurs

External Issues:

- Turnover may disrupt team

The team posts its information on the storyboard (see Figure 12), and is ready to move on to Step 2.

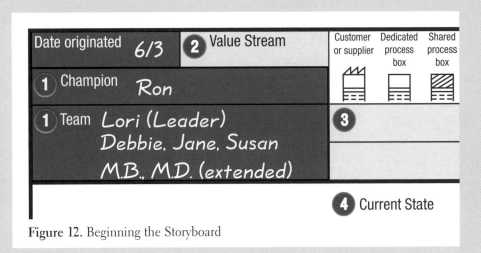

Figure 12. Beginning the Storyboard

Step 2. Choose the Value Stream

What Is a Value Stream?

Companies survive only when they provide goods and services that are of value to their customers. The flow of information and materials (work units) to produce that value is what we call a value stream. A value stream consists of:

- Everything, including non-value-adding activities, that makes the transformation from raw information and materials to what the customer is willing to pay for.

- Communication all along the supply chain regarding orders and order forecasts.

- The network of processes and operations through which *materials and information flow*, in time and space, as they are being transformed.

> ### Why Do We Call It a Value Stream?
>
> **Value** assumes that you are creating something of value that a customer is willing to pay for.
>
> **Stream** refers to a sequential flow of activities needed to create work units and deliver them to the customer.

Just as many rivers flow into an ocean, there are many value streams within an organization. A value stream encompasses all the actions (both value-added and non-value-added) that are necessary to bring a product or service from the original concept through the development and/or manufacturing processes to the receipt of payment. In manufacturing, each product family follows a separate value stream. A product family is typically a group of parts or part numbers that share a common processing sequence.

For each product family, there are three areas of the value stream that overlap and flow together:[1]

1. The concept-to-launch (administrative) area.

2. The raw material-to-finished product (manufacturing) area.

3. The order-to-cash (administrative) area.

Each area of the value stream includes multiple processes and activities (see Figure 13).

---

1. James P. Womak and Daniel T. Jones. *Lean Thinking: Banish Waste and Create Wealth in Your Corporation*. New York: Simon & Schuster, 1996.

Three Areas of the Value Stream

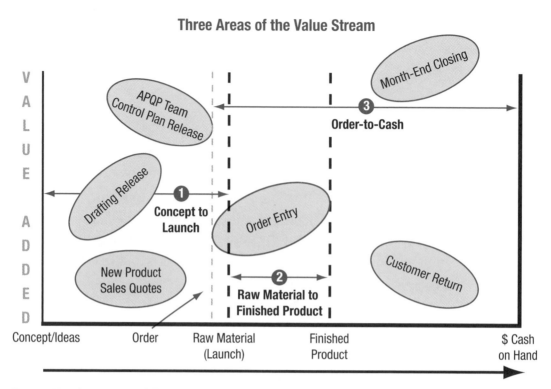

Figure 13. Three Areas of the Value Stream

Concept to Launch

The administrative or office areas of a value stream in a manufacturing company often begin with the documentation required for a part to be manufactured (e.g., prints, drawings, routers, control plans). There are many processes in the concept-to-launch value stream, including the drafting release process, the pricing process, the procurement process, engineering proposals, customer ordering and quoting prior to production, and the control plan release process.

> *Concept-to-Launch Processes*
>
> • Drafting release process
>
> • Pricing
>
> • Procurement
>
> • Engineering proposals
>
> • Customer ordering and quotes
>
> • Control plan release process

It should be noted that these processes are not separate value streams. They are processes *within* a value stream. One of the biggest mistakes people make is to attempt to improve individual processes without a complete picture of a value stream. Don't do it! Understand your value stream first. Create a plan for improvement. *Then* improve individual processes relative to the value stream based on that plan.

Raw Material to Finished Product

This area of the value stream contains all the manufacturing material and information requirements to deliver the product to the customer with the highest quality, lowest cost, and shortest lead time.[2]

Order to Cash

This area of the value stream begins with the incoming customer order, which is usually received through the sales department, customer service, or via e-commerce and ends with the receipt of payment. Depending on the flow of the manufacturing process, there may be some overlap with the raw material-to-finished product value stream.

A few examples of processes within the order-to-cash value stream are: order lead-time process, customer service returned material reports, contested invoices, month-end closing, drafting revision process, and product enhancement process.

Order-to-Cash Processes

- Order lead-time process
- Customer service returned material reports
- Contested invoices
- Month-end closing
- New hire application process
- Drafting revision process
- Product enhancement process
- Capital authorization request process

Remember that between 60 and 80 percent of the costs associated with a product line are nonproduction costs. These nonproduction, administrative processes are supposed to ensure that the product is ordered, released, shipped, and paid for. They play a crucial role in maintaining your business. They also provide an enormous, but often overlooked, opportunity for improvement. The goal of lean management is not to eliminate those functions; it is to make the process more visual and significantly more efficient by utilizing lean principles.

Always remember this about lean management: the purpose of the lean management process is not to make someone *work faster*, but rather to streamline the flow to have the work *move faster* through the value stream.

---

2. The companion book to this one, *Value Stream Management*, by Don Tapping, Tom Luyster, and Tom Shuker, and the video training program entitled *Value Stream Management: Eight Steps to Planning, Mapping, and Sustaining Lean Improvements*, by Don Tapping and Tom Fabrizio, address the management of this type of value stream in depth from the manufacturing perspective.

How to Choose a Value Stream for Improvement

Overall value streams can be difficult to tackle due to their complexity. Therefore, the three overall value stream areas will be broken down into smaller streams. The key to targeting a smaller value stream for improvement is to look beyond an individual process (say creating a drawing) towards the upstream and downstream processes that are impacted. By looking at upstream and downstream processes that share similar characteristics (i.e., people, functions, databases), economies of scale can be created when implementing a lean initiative.

There are times when the choice of a target value stream for improvement is simple — your external customer demands it of you. If one of your primary customers is Clubs, and they are unhappy with order lead time, then *order processing for Clubs* is your target value stream.

Or, consider an e-commerce company where customers are satisfied with the time it takes to receive an order, but management wants to use product shipping time to create a distinct advantage over the competition. An order received through a website can be seen as a "part" or work unit to add value to in the administrative value stream. The order travels through many processes, from receiving to order processing to delivery to payment, and the entire value stream for that order needs to be mapped out and analyzed so it can be improved.

There are four main activities involved in choosing a value stream:

   1. Identify any immediate customer concerns.

   2. Perform a work-unit routing analysis.

   3. Prioritize target value streams.

   4. Update your team charter and continue catchball.

The Work-Unit Routing Analysis

If a customer does not immediately identify a target value stream for you, you can use work-unit routing analysis. By creating a chart showing which work units, families of work units, or customers travel through the same sequence of administrative procedures or processes, you can identify separate value streams as candidates for the target value stream for your project. Then you can make your decision based on importance or volume.

To perform a work-unit routing analysis, follow these steps (refer to the example in Figure 14):

   1. Start by listing in a column the families of work units or customers that are involved in the general area you are targeting for improvement (refer to your VSM team charter).

   2. In the next column, show the average volume of work performed for each family or customer within a given time period.

   3. List across the top of the sheet the sequence of processes or activities performed for all the families or customers you have specified.

4. Indicate which processes or activities apply to each family or customer by marking X's in the grid.

5. Group together the families or customers that have the same process routes, and rank them by volume.

Work-Unit Routing Analysis					
Work-Unit Type	Average Work Volume (monthly)	Process A	Process B	Process C	Process D
X	500	X	X	X	
Y	175		X		X
Z	20	X	X	X	

Figure 14. Work-Unit Routing Analysis

In Figure 14 you would group work unit types X and Z as a target value stream due to the volume of work and common process routes. If Z did not have the common processes, then X would be the identified value stream, sequenced by volume.

Keys to Successful Implementation

In order to successfully complete Step 2, the core implementation team must do the following.

1. Listen to the customer.

In the early stages of value stream management for the lean office you cannot solve every one of your problems, and you cannot improve every one of your value streams. You must be selective. Being selective means solving the problems demanded by your customers first. Often your customers, either internal or external, can tell you where to look for the value stream family that most needs improvement.

2. Understand the picture within your walls.

Even though a value stream represents the complete path within the walls of a facility, and even travels across plants from customer to producer, it is best to begin within your own building. So in the beginning phases of VSM, the target value stream that you select should begin and end within the boundaries of your facility. For instance, let's say you can return a customer quote within two weeks. However, you have realized that your competitor can do it within a day. To remain competitive and stay in business, you must focus on the quoting process. This would entail creating a value stream consisting of pricing and marketing (customer service, engineering, payables, etc.). And let's not forget IT. For this type of improvement you need to build a cross-functional team to follow this value stream. Each department or function would work within the VSM process to create a lean quoting value stream. Rarely could this be completed within each function independently.

At the same time, your target value stream shouldn't be too small. Without a complete "big picture" you won't understand where the waste really is and where the potential for improvement exists.

3. Ensure that the value stream touches the ultimate customer.

It is important to have the value stream "touch," or relate to, the ultimate customer. You will find it easier to justify resource commitment if you are improving in order to identify and meet a customer's direct need.

4. Get buy-in from managers.

Once the core implementation team has targeted a value stream, it must perform one more task before moving to Step 3 ("Learn about Lean"). That task is to get buy-in from the project champion or other managers with a stake in the value stream. The catchball approach will ensure management commitment and prevent problems later.

PREMIERE CASE STUDY—STEP 2

The team decided that the entire customer service department value stream needed to be lean, but to tackle it all at once would be impossible. They decided to determine a value stream on which to improve.

Since orders from different customers followed different processing routes, the team decided to analyze orders from different customers in order to choose a value stream. The team first listed the customers (or customer groups) responsible for orders (see Figure 15). They listed customers by volume, with the highest volume first. In the second column the team listed the percentage of orders that each customer was responsible for over the past 12 weeks.

Next, the team identified the sequence of processes that an order might take. They listed those processes across the top, one process per column. The most extensive possible sequence is as follows:

- Central mail sort, to
- Sales mail sort, to
- Initiate order, to
- Check part numbers, to
- Assign delivery date, to
- Verify order, to

- Sales mail sort, to
- Central mail sort

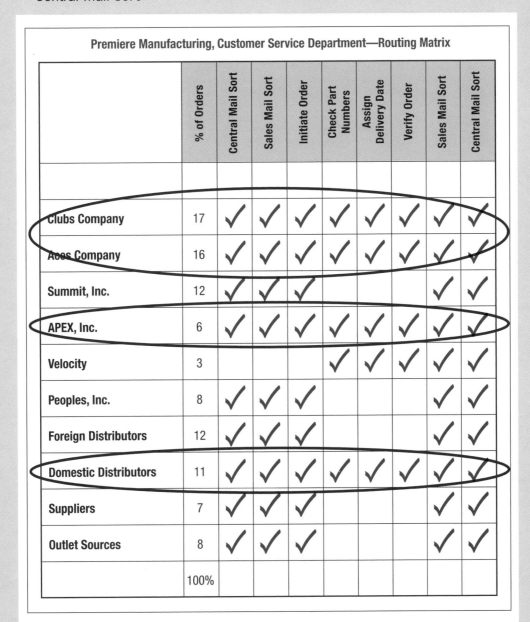

Premiere Manufacturing, Customer Service Department—Routing Matrix

	% of Orders	Central Mail Sort	Sales Mail Sort	Initiate Order	Check Part Numbers	Assign Delivery Date	Verify Order	Sales Mail Sort	Central Mail Sort
Clubs Company	17	✓	✓	✓	✓	✓	✓	✓	✓
Aces Company	16	✓	✓	✓	✓	✓	✓	✓	✓
Summit, Inc.	12	✓	✓	✓				✓	✓
APEX, Inc.	6	✓	✓	✓	✓	✓	✓	✓	✓
Velocity	3				✓	✓	✓	✓	✓
Peoples, Inc.	8	✓	✓	✓				✓	✓
Foreign Distributors	12	✓	✓	✓				✓	✓
Domestic Distributors	11	✓	✓	✓	✓	✓	✓	✓	✓
Suppliers	7	✓	✓	✓				✓	✓
Outlet Sources	8	✓	✓	✓				✓	✓
	100%								

Figure 15. Premiere's Work-Unit Routing Analysis Matrix

From the matrix it was easy to construct three family groups (see Figure 16) because of the flow they follow within the value stream. Velocity remained its own family.

Premiere's Three Value Streams

Family I	Family II	Family III
Clubs Company	Summit, Inc.	Velocity
Aces Company	Peoples, Inc.	
APEX, Inc.	Foreign Distributors	
Domestic Distributors	Suppliers	
	Outlet Sources	

Figure 16. Premiere's Three Value Streams

For their first project the team decided to work on Family I orders because they accounted for 50 percent of all orders received. They notified the champion of their decision to narrow their focus, and the champion agreed with the decision.

The champion also noted that this decision should have a helpful effect on the other customer processes as well, which reaffirmed his support.

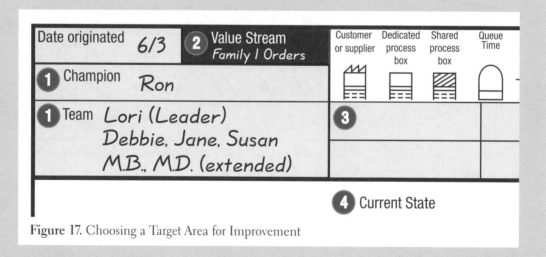

Figure 17. Choosing a Target Area for Improvement

Step 3. Learn About Lean

In Steps 1 and 2 you gained management commitment, formed a core implementation team, and identified the value stream targeted for lean conversion. Before you can map the current state (Step 4), identify lean metrics (Step 5), and map the future state (Step 6), you must gain a good understanding of lean concepts and terms. The purpose of Step 3 is to ensure that everyone has this understanding.

This step covers some key points on how to approach the training, and then reviews the lean concepts that should be conveyed during the training. As you read about each concept or tool, keep in mind that this is only one avenue or approach to learning about lean. The learning and implementation process is different for every organization. Here we document a proven approach that has worked in many organizations throughout the world, but it is by no means the only way. Take what makes good business sense for your organization and integrate it.

Training and Doing—The Balancing Act

There is a delicate balance between training and doing. Lean concepts must make good business sense *now*, before going to the next step. But ideally you will want to utilize the "LEAP" approach to all training:

LEarn . . . and then . . . APply

The faster the *AP* follows the *LE*, the better the results. You will learn a lot once you start creating and implementing. But if people are not asking questions, or if they seem disinterested, reconsider the approach immediately before you go any further. More training or explanation on lean concepts and tools may be necessary.

Learning the lean system is a lot like learning to ride a bicycle. It is something that cannot be done entirely in a classroom or by reading a book. You can draw a bicycle on a white board and tell people where to place their hands, where to sit, and where to put their feet. But this explanation is not enough to teach someone how to ride a bike. To become proficient at riding a bike, you have to *get on the bike and ride it.* You may need some assistance at first, because you haven't yet learned how to balance. After several attempts and falls, however, you start to understand the requirements and develop a sense or feel for riding.

Understanding and implementing the lean system is very similar. You can read material about the system and attend workshops and conferences on the subject. This will help, but like riding a bicycle, you must learn by *doing*. Similarly, you will need some assistance in the beginning from people who have implemented before. They can help you keep your balance. You can now begin to change your workplace with kaizen events. You will make mistakes; don't give up when that happens. Pick yourself up and try again.

Remember that the goal of learning is to get to the *doing* in Step 8. The point of a lean office transformation is to drive waste from the value stream. If you put a great deal of effort into planning a transformation, but then the transformation doesn't actually occur, all the time and effort that went into the planning is wasted.

Creating a Learning Plan

All companies aspiring to become lean must place a premium on education and training. To get the core implementation team up to speed, develop a training plan based on the following six steps:

1. Determine the required skills and knowledge.

2. Assess current skill and knowledge levels of team members.

3. Determine the gap between present skills and knowledge and required skills and knowledge.

4. Design the training.

5. Schedule and conduct the training.

6. Evaluate the effectiveness of the training.

Be sure to document the plan by making a specific agenda of activities, listing who will participate, and setting target completion dates.

The knowledge for the training should come from a variety of sources. Some good options for training include:

• Conducting a simulation that ties all the lean concepts together. This can be accomplished by attending a public workshop or using materials your training department may supply.

• Benchmarking another facility that is using some of the tools.

• Demonstrating a successful in-house project.

• Using internal resources to conduct "just-in-time" lean training sessions that are quickly followed by actual application of the concepts.

• Using a consultant to facilitate the learning as it relates to the value stream.

• Using books and videos combined with group discussion of the content.

The more you learn and do regarding lean, the more you will be able to learn and do. As with everything, real learning is cumulative; the way to gain experience with a lean office is in small, incremental steps. Build from what works and move on.

> ### *Benchmarking*
>
> Benchmarking is a structured approach to identifying a world-class process, then gathering relevant information and applying it within your own organization to improve a similar process.
>
> ### *Benchmarking Guidelines*
>
> ❑ **Be specific.** Be specific in defining what you want to improve. You may want to improve your entire administrative operation, but you also may want to see specifically how a company uses supermarket concepts and kanbans.
>
> ❑ **Be willing to share.** Identify an area you think may be world class in your organization, if you can, and present that to the potential benchmark site as something you are willing to share with them.
>
> ❑ **Make it win-win.** Attempt to make it a win-win experience. Identify what's in it for them! Offer something. Let them know that you are sincere.
>
> ❑ **Know the site.** Ensure that the benchmark team is familiar with some aspects of the company you will benchmark (what it produces or sells, size, etc.).
>
> ❑ **Send questions.** Fax or e-mail specific questions in advance to the benchmark company's point person.
>
> ❑ **Don't go alone.** Do not benchmark in isolation. It is always better to have a minimum of two members on the benchmarking team.
>
> ❑ **Document.** Document and take notes as needed.
>
> ❑ **Respect privacy.** If some information is proprietary and cannot be released, respect that and move on.
>
> ❑ **Dress appropriately.** Be sure to discuss attire prior to the visit. Most companies have a "business-casual" dress code, but make sure you never underdress.
>
> ❑ **Call them.** Consider conference calling if an on-site visit is not practical.
>
> ❑ **Say "thanks"—a lot.** Show appreciation to the benchmarking site host. Consider giving some company t-shirts, hats, or golf balls to the people you will be visiting.
>
> ❑ **Follow up.** Follow up with a letter to the host facility detailing what you found helpful. Again, offer to be a benchmark site for them at any time in the future.

Key Concepts of Lean

What exactly do we mean when we talk about lean? A lean system is one in which people strive to eliminate non-value-adding activities, or waste. In the remainder of this chapter, we will briefly identify the various tools utilized within the lean approach. They will be further utilized and explained as they relate to the Premiere case study in Steps, 4, 5 and 6.

What do employees need to know before embarking on a transformation to a lean system? The key concepts in understanding lean are:

- The cost reduction principle
- The seven deadly wastes
- Just-in-time
- Three phases of lean application:
  - Customer demand phase
  - Continuous flow phase
  - Leveling phase
- Total employee involvement
- The visual office

The Cost Reduction Principle

Traditional management thinking dictates that you set your sale price by calculating your cost and adding on a margin of profit. But in today's economic environment this is a problem. There is always someone ready to take your place.

Lean evolved out of Toyota's cost reduction philosophy. In that approach, market conditions (i.e., customers) set the selling price, and cost and profit become variables. The primary focus is on internal costs.

Using the cost reduction approach, you determine the price customers are willing to pay and subtract your cost to determine your profit at that cost level (see Figure 18). This "lean thinking"—that price – cost = profit—forces you to reduce costs within the organization to ensure profit. That is why it is so important to look at reducing waste as the primary method of maximizing your profits.

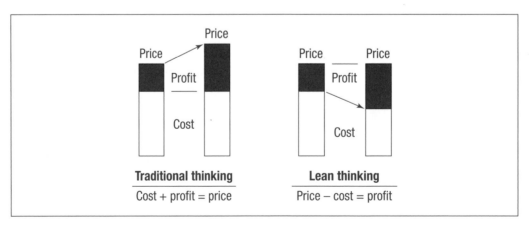

Figure 18. Cost Plus versus Price Minus

So in lean, when we say *"The customer is first"* we really mean it—even to the level of determining our cost and profit, and by extension, how efficient we will be.

The Seven Deadly Wastes

How can office workers reduce and maintain costs on a daily basis? It's just not reasonable to have everyone being a part-time bookkeeper. However, everyone *can* wage war on the seven deadly wastes.

Waste

The ultimate lean target is the total elimination of waste. In lean terms, waste is anything that adds cost or time without adding value. It is something being done that has no value to customers even though it may be included in the overall cost.

Prior methods of process improvement have looked at waste from a departmental perspective, without clearly defining specifics. This approach made it extremely difficult to get a handle on dealing with waste. Waste is often hidden in processes, which makes it difficult to detect. Lean breaks waste down into specific aspects to allow easier identification for focused improvement activities.

Waste is categorized into seven different types. Each can be targeted specifically to help identify the appropriate lean tool to assist in its elimination. To date, the focus of waste reduction has been primarily on the shopfloor, in manufacturing processes.

Waste is even more of a problem in the office. A disorganized, wasteful environment exacts a heavy toll on people. It keeps them from being and feeling successful.

Wastes are known as the seven deadly wastes because they are like toxins in the work environment. The first step toward eliminating them is to be able to recognize them for what they are. Let's review the seven deadly wastes.

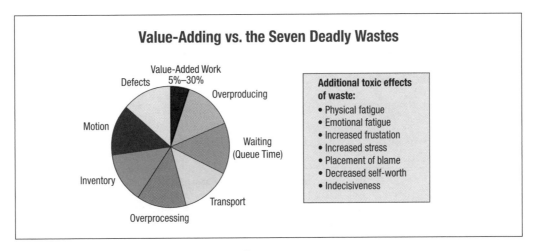

Figure 19. Value-Adding vs. the Seven Deadly Wastes

1. The waste of overproducing.

When you overproduce you produce too much of something or produce it before it is required. In the manufacturing environment, units are overproduced. In the office, it is more likely to be paper and information.

Producing more than needed or producing it too soon does not improve efficiency. It consumes resources, such as materials, people, and storage, faster than necessary and brings about other kinds of waste.

> ### *To eliminate this type of waste:
>
> - Establish a work flow sequence to satisfy the downstream customer.
> - Create workplace norms and standards for each process.
> - Create signal devices to prevent early processing.

2. The waste of waiting.

Waiting for anything—people, paper, machines or information—is waste. Waiting means idle time, and that causes the workflow to stop. It adds no value to the work unit or service, and the customer certainly doesn't want to pay for it.

The waste of waiting is the easiest to detect. It is also the most aggravating to employees. There are many examples in the office: waiting for signatures, waiting for machines, waiting for phone calls, waiting for supplies.

> ### To eliminate this type of waste:
>
> - Review and standardize required signatures to eliminate unnecessary ones.
> - Cross-train employees to allow work flow to continue while someone is out.
> - Balance the workload throughout the day to ensure that all people are being used optimally.
> - Make sure that equipment and supplies are available.

3. The waste of overprocessing.

Waste is associated with processing things that the customer doesn't want (and therefore doesn't want to pay for). The waste of overprocessing often includes redundant activities such as checking someone else's work, obtaining multiple signatures, or excessive reviews.

> ### To eliminate this type of waste:
>
> - Review the value-added steps in each process, and streamline or eliminate steps whenever possible.
> - Review all signature requirements and eliminate signatures wherever possible.

4. The waste of inventory.

Excess stock of anything is waste. Excess inventory takes up space, may impact safety, and can become obsolete if work requirements change. Unneeded files, extra supplies, and unnecessary copies are some types of inventory waste. The waste of inventory can be a departmental matter, or it can be an individual one (How many pads of post-its do *you* squirrel away in your desk?).

The waste of inventory is a habit that may be difficult to break. Extra inventory represents a margin of safety that we may be unwilling to let go of. Lean thinking means changing this mindset.

Having extra supplies means you have more to manage. Extra inventory can obstruct other processes as well: if you are looking for another item, you have to move extra inventory, resulting in a waste of motion. Or, if it is improperly lifted, it can be a safety issue. Finally, things may become obsolete before you get around to using them.

A critical point: we also relate this waste to time. *Time is a valuable commodity in the office environment, and a work unit or folder sitting on someone's desk is waste.*

To eliminate this type of waste:

- Produce only enough to satisfy the work requirements of your downstream customer.

- Standardize work locations and the number of units per location.

- Ensure that work arrives at the downstream process when it is required and does not sit there.

---

5. The waste of motion.

Any motion that is not necessary to the successful completion of an operation is waste. All unnecessary work movements are a form of waste. All motion should add value to the work unit or service for the customer. Ineffective job processes and layout are often responsible for creating more walking, reaching, or bending than are necessary.

To eliminate this type of waste:

- Standardize folders, drawers, and cabinets throughout the area; use color codes as much as possible.

- Arrange your files (desktop and electronic on PC) in such a way you can easily reference them.

- Arrange work areas of office equipment in central locations; consider purchasing additional equipment to eliminate multiple trips.

---

6. The waste of defects or correction.

Waste arising from producing defective work that needs to be redone is clearly waste. Doing something over is waste. This waste also includes productivity losses associated with disrupting a normal process to deal with defects or rework. The waste of correction is much easier to spot than many other forms of waste.

> ***To eliminate this type of waste:***
>
> • Establish standardized work procedures and office forms.
>
> • Create and post job aids.

7. The waste of transport.

Transporting something farther than necessary, or temporarily locating, filing, stocking, stacking, or moving materials, people, information or paper, wastes time and energy. Materials and supplies are often moved several times before reaching a permanent location. All of this movement is waste. In addition, things in temporary storage are more likely to be broken, stolen, lost, or become an obstruction.

> ***To eliminate this type of waste:***
>
> • Make the distance over which something is moved as short as possible.
>
> • Eliminate any temporary storage locations or stocking locations.

Once you understand waste and where to find it, it's not difficult to see the logic in lean. Use lean to slash waste and increase value-added work. Let's start by looking at just-in-time systems.

Just-in-Time

Just-in-time is at the heart of the lean system. It ensures that, during work, the next downstream process has:

• Only those work units needed.

• Just when they are needed

• In the exact amount needed

The ideal state is characterized by the ability to replenish a single work unit when the customer has pulled it (i.e., it has been pulled by the downstream process). This ideal state is also referred to as a "pull system." This is the opposite of a "push system," common in most workplaces, in which work piles up in batches as it is pushed from process to process.

To accomplish this state, understand that the people with the most important information are your colleagues in the process downstream of you. They are the ones who can tell you what they need, when they need it, in the exact amount needed.

In the office, we are concerned with the flow of various types of work units as well as information. Applying lean principles in the office means learning to see the flow of business processes in terms of units of work or information (see Figure 20).

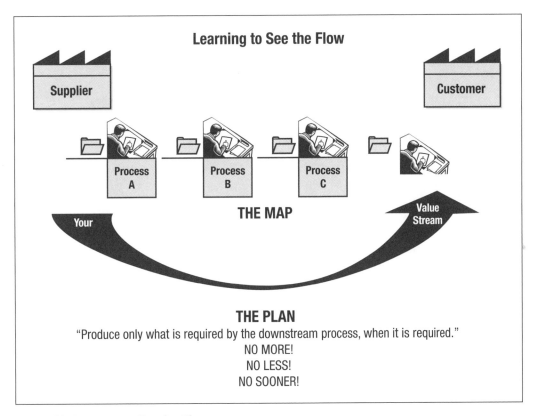

Figure 20. Learning to See the Flow

Three Phases of Lean Application

It is helpful to group lean concepts into three phases: customer demand, continuous flow, and leveling (see Figure 21).

We recommend that you implement these phases in the same order that you learn about them. (Remember, one of the main reasons why lean transformations fail to be sustained is that people have "cherry picked" the implementation tools, including the popular kaizen workshops and value stream mapping workshops.) Understanding the demand, flow, and leveling phases of application, along with the guidelines for implementing the VSM process, will give you the solid approach required, not only for implementing but also for sustaining lean improvements.

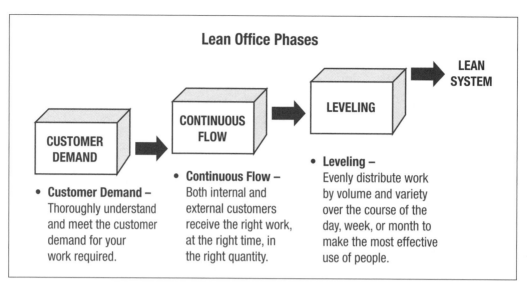

Figure 21. Three Phases of Lean Application

Customer Demand Phase

First, you must determine who the customer is and what the customer's requirements are. You will then be in a position to meet customer demand. The various tools and concepts for determining and meeting demand include:

- Takt time calculation
- Pitch calculation
- Buffer and safety resources
- 5S for the office
- Problem-solving methods

We will explore these tools and concepts in Step 6–Phase I

Continuous Flow Phase

Secondly, you must establish continuous flow to ensure that the right work units arrive at the right time, in the correct amounts, to your customers—both internal and external. In Step 6–Phase II we will explore the following in some detail.

- In-process supermarkets
- Kanban system
- FIFO
- Line balancing
- Standardized work
- Work area design

Leveling Phase

Finally, after you have determined demand and set up continuous flow, you must perform leveling to distribute work evenly and effectively. In Step 6–Phase III we will review:

- Visible pitch board
- Load leveling (heijunka) box
- Runner system

The lean approach is a powerful force for change and growth. Sustaining daily growth depends on establishing two important foundations: total employee involvement and a visual office.

Total Employee Involvement

Every house needs a firm foundation. In a lean system the foundation for everything begins with your philosophy about people. Employees should be encouraged to make positive contributions to improving their own work areas. Through kaizen events, teams meet for a short period to analyze a problem, recommend an improvement activity, and make it happen, allowing continuous improvement ideas to become a reality.

Kaizen

Small daily improvements performed by everyone. The word "kaizen" comes from the Japanese characters "kai," to take apart, and "zen," to make good. The point of kaizen implementation is the total elimination of waste.

World-class factories are best known for the thousands of informal kaizens that occur on a daily basis. And it is through total employee involvement that these activities can succeed.

Thousands of books have been written about the role of people in lean, but there are a few basic principles that must exist for you to succeed:

- **No-blame.** Problem solving and improvement focuses on the work, not the people.
- **Teamwork.** A team is much greater than the sum of its parts.
- **Vision.** Each person needs to have a greater view than just the work in front of him or her. Seeing the value stream will fill that requirement.
- **Catchball.** Getting feedback, buy-in, and new ideas is an ongoing activity. Always share ideas with your managers and the people who work for you.
- **Continuous improvement.** Everyone should be encouraged to improve.
- **Ownership.** Everyone needs to feel a part of the event and care about the outcome.

The Visual Office

The visual office begins with one simple premise: "A picture is worth a thousand words"—especially if that picture conveys exactly what you need, when and where you need it. The goal of the visual office is to give people control of the workplace. The visual office contributes to total employee involvement. It entails the following actions:

- A designated place to share improvement ideas that is common to the area.
- A system to maintain visual standards and levels of housekeeping (a 5S program).
- A small team that is rotated on a regular basis to continually improve.

The benefits of maintaining a visual office are:

- Promotes communication throughout the department.
- Allows visitors to get a sense of what is happening in an area.
- Allows for a sense of pride to workers.
- Demonstrates a process of continual improvement.

Keys to Successful Implementation

In order to complete Step 3 successfully, you must:

1. Create a training plan that makes sense for your organization.

Everyone has different needs, budgets, and resources. Every group of people has a different set of knowledge. The training plan should fit your set of knowledge.

After seeing what you need, see what is available to you in your company. You may have a lean expert at home—take advantage of local resources.

2. Use a variety of sources and materials for the training.

People don't learn in just one way. Some people like to learn by reading, others by watching. Your plan has to include the major learning methods for most people, which are:

- Books, videos, and study groups
- Conferences, seminars, and lectures
- Courses and workshops

3. Gather information and ideas through benchmarking.

Learning to think in lean terms means learning to think creatively. It's important to go beyond the walls of your own workplace—and even outside your own industry—to observe how things are done and how you might adapt ideas to fit your system. A classic example is the supermarket concept for in-process work, which we'll talk about in Step 6.

PREMIERE CASE STUDY—STEP 3

The team creates a training plan and spends the next six weeks learning about lean tools and methods (see Figure 22).

Premiere Manufacturing Lean Training Plan

Team Member	Training Activity	Completed By
Debbie	Attend Overview/Simulation Benchmark Company C Attend Lean Workshop	6/15 6/30 7/15
Jane	Attend Overview/Simulation Benchmark Company C	6/15 6/30
Lori (Team Leader)	Attend Overview/Simulation Benchmark Company C Read *Lean Thinking* Read *Value Stream Management*	6/15 6/30 7/30 7/30
Ron (Champion)	Attend Overview/Simulation Benchmark Company C	6/15 6/30
Susan	Attend Overview/Simulation Benchmark Company C Attend Lean Workshop	6/15 6/30 7/15

Figure 22. Premiere Manufacturing Lean Training Plan

The entire team attends a four-hour overview on lean techniques conducted by Premiere's training department. The overview includes a lean simulation that demonstrates the benefits of continuous flow. The team also goes on a benchmarking trip to a local company that has successfully implemented lean office methods. Two of the members attend a one-day workshop on lean. The team leader completes and gives a report on *Lean Thinking*, by Womack and Jones.

After discussing what they have learned and observed, the team members conclude that the target value stream is operating with very limited continuous flow. The work areas are generally disorganized and disorderly, and there is tremendous variation in the way different workers in the department perform value-adding tasks. The team enters these observations on the storyboard and looks forward to mapping the current state in Step 4.

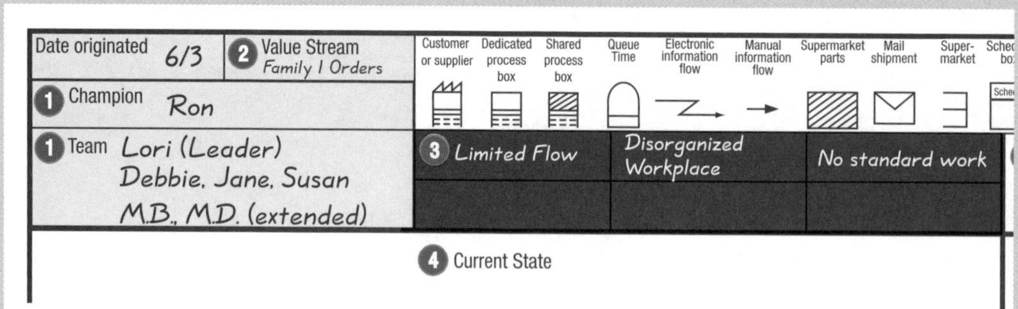

Figure 23. Listing Problems in the Target Area

Step 4. Map the Current State

After attaining a good understanding of lean, the next step is to map the current state, showing the flow of work units and information by using a set of symbols or "icons." Because a value stream map is a visual representation of material and information flow for a particular value stream, it is indispensable as a tool for visually managing process improvements.

To improve a value stream, of course, you must first observe and understand it. Mapping the process gives you a clear picture of the wastes that inhibit flow. Eliminating the waste makes it possible to reduce administrative processing time, which will help you consistently meet customer demand.

In creating your map you should focus on having your core team gather accurate, real-time data related to your product family and its value streams and use this information to identify all the specific activities occuring along each value stream.

When collecting data for your current-state map, start from the closest point to the customer and work your way upstream through the various processes as shown below. This will help you observe and understand the value stream from your customer's perspective.

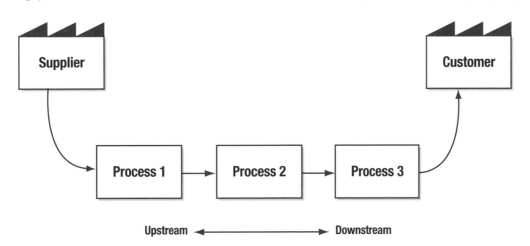

Start your map with the customer (on the right side) and move upstream (toward the left).

This mapping step is divided into two parts. The first part is preparing to map, followed by the drawing of the map. Each part will be reviewed.

In general, answering simple questions such as, "Where does the work originate, or where does it come from?" and conveying that information on a sheet of paper with standard icons is all there is to value stream mapping your current state. But do not underestimate the importance of accurate information. Remember to begin at the downstream process closest to the customer, either internal or external. Take your time!

Preparing to Map the Current State

There are four steps to preparation:

1. **Determine individual assignments** to ensure that everyone knows his or her part in this step. You need some, if not all, of the following roles assigned:
   - Scribe to draw on a flipchart or whiteboard
   - Facilitator to keep everything on schedule
   - Timekeeper to be responsible for collecting accurate cycle times and queue times (and any other relevant data)

   There may be other roles, but assigning these three will get you off to a good start.

2. **Determine the main processes** and draw rough sketches of the entire value stream with the team. Do this on a white board in a conference room, as a team. This will confirm to everyone exactly where you will begin to collect your data and make sure that everyone has the same value stream perspective. You may be surprised to find that what is *supposed* to exist doesn't exist, but things that never seemed possible *do* exist.

3. **Go to where the action is**, beginning with the most downstream process. Always collect the actual process data (or attributes). Always collect the following data:
   - Total time per workday.
   - Regularly planned downtime (meetings, lunch, breaks, etc.).
   - Available time (subtract regularly planned downtime from total available time).
   - Number of people working in the process.
   - Quantity of work performed in one day by one person.
   - Frequency at which work is delivered to the next process.
   - Cycle time (the time that elapses from the beginning of a process or operation until its completion).
   - Queue time (the amount of time a work unit will wait before a downstream process is ready to work on it).
   - Exceptions to the process. These need to be addressed by the team at some point. For instance, one process may claim that someone from sales always disrupts them by requesting a special "hot" quote. This happens every day and consumes one hour. This would be noted and discussed with the team.

   Each value stream is different, so the team should prepare a list of process attributes before they begin.

Additional Administrative Attributes

- Delivery schedules (mail, etc.)
- Reliability mistakes
- Computer and equipment issues
- Work disruptions
- Square footage
- Distance traveled for jobs
- Information flow

---

4. Briefly discuss the data *away* from the work area once all the data has been collected.

Research Etiquette

Whenever you go to where the action is, be sure to do the following:

- Get management approval and involvement.
- Communicate to all areas before going there.
- Make proper introductions when you get there.
- Explain your purpose.
- Be open and honest when responding to questions.
- Respect people's workspace.
- Remember that the people who work there are the experts.

Throughout the data-collection process, remember that you are gathering information relating only to the identified value stream. When you have compiled data, you will be ready to map the current state. First, however, take some time to review the icons used in mapping the value stream (see Figure 24).

How to Draw the Current-State Map

Now that you have seen where the action is and gathered the data, you are ready to create a current-state map. Always begin with a blank board or piece of paper, and write in erasable pen or pencil.

This is a generic current-state mapping procedure. You should always begin here, then modify your procedure to fit the needs of your value stream.

1. Draw the external (or internal) customer and the supplier (if the supplier is different from the customer) and list their requirements

2. Draw the entry and exit processes to the value stream.

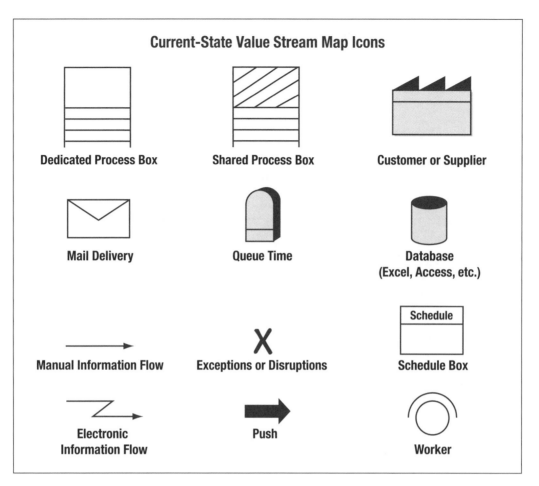

Figure 24. Current-State Value Stream Map Icons

3. Draw all processes between the entry and exit processes beginning farthest downstream.

4. List all process attributes.

5. Draw queue times between processes.

6. Draw all communications that occur within the value stream.

7. Draw push or pull icons to identify the type of workflow.

8. Complete the map with any other data.

Remember, all value streams are different. After learning how to use this sequence we encourage you to modify and adapt—except for one part. Always start with your customer!

To understand the creation of a current-state map, follow along with the Premiere team as they map the current state.

PREMIERE CASE STUDY—STEP 4

In Step 2, the core implementation team at Premiere Manufacturing chose to focus on the value stream for orders for three customers (Clubs, Aces and Apex), along with the domestic distributors (identified as value stream Family I). In Step 3, the team received a comprehensive overview of lean concepts. Now the team is ready to map the current state.

Preparing to Map the Current State

1. Determine individual assignments.

The team met and assigned one person as the scribe to write down the process steps and work elements, one person as the designated timekeeper to measure actual cycle times, and one person as the spokesperson for the team as they walked the flow and collected data. Even though this team was experienced within the various areas of customer service, they realized that this was the most efficient way of gathering current and accurate data.

2. Determine the main processes.

The team determined that the main process areas for an order for Family I, and the personnel within each area, were as follows (see Figure 25):

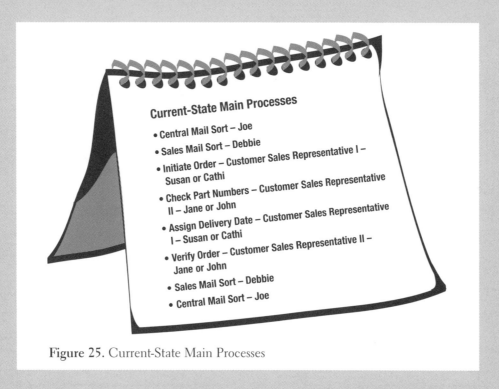

Current-State Main Processes

- Central Mail Sort – Joe
- Sales Mail Sort – Debbie
- Initiate Order – Customer Sales Representative I – Susan or Cathi
- Check Part Numbers – Customer Sales Representative II – Jane or John
- Assign Delivery Date – Customer Sales Representative I – Susan or Cathi
- Verify Order – Customer Sales Representative II – Jane or John
- Sales Mail Sort – Debbie
- Central Mail Sort – Joe

Figure 25. Current-State Main Processes

3. Go to where the action is.

The team collected a great deal of data (shown in Premiere Attributes, below) about the activities occurring in the main process areas, the cycle times for each activity, the means by which information was conveyed, and the main exceptions to the normal flow of orders, including expedited orders and returned work units.

4. Briefly discuss the data.

The team went back to their meeting room to discuss the data. They then decided to map the current state by following an average order through the value stream.

The customer service reps decided to capture the customer data for four weeks. They wanted to determine the average order by number of line items. Each customer service rep had a data checksheet and marked off how many line items for each customer were on each order. Below is a compilation of the data.

Customer service processed 540 orders during the four weeks for the four customers. Total line items for those orders were 8,100. The average number of line items per order was determined to be 15 [8,100 ÷ 540 = 15].

Date	Number of Orders	Number of Line Items
Week 1	169	2078
Week 2	99	1701
Week 3	114	1798
Week 4	158	2523
Totals	540	8100

Premiere Attributes

Customer attributes:

- Customer mail (orders, returned work units) is received at 8:00 a.m., 12:00 p.m., and 3:00 p.m. in the central mailroom.
- Customer faxes orders to the sales mailroom
- Customer phones in expedited orders to customer sales representative I
- Customer receives a faxed order acknowledgment from customer sales representative I after it has been approved by customer sales representative II
- Customer receives an order acknowledgment from the central mailroom
- Customer requests that orders be processed within 24 hours of receipt

Central mail sort:

- Central mailroom receives the outside mail at 8:00 a.m., 12:00 p.m., and 3:00 p.m. daily
- Central mailroom attendant (Joe) sorts the mail to all departments (five seconds per order or fax) and places mail in outbox (five seconds per order or fax)
- Mail is delivered to the sales mailroom at 9:00 a.m. daily
- Eight-hour queue time to downstream process

Sales mail sort:

- Debbie sorts mail by customer (five seconds/order), date-stamps mail (two seconds/order), places orders in folders for CSRs (10 seconds/order), and delivers folders to CSR I once daily at 1:00 p.m.
- Four-hour queue time

Initiate order:

- CSR I (Susan or Cathi) initiates the order by computer—45 seconds/line item
- Handles returned work units 4 minutes per order (this is an exception)
- Expedites orders—10 minutes per order (this is an exception)
- Delivers order folders by foot to customer service representative II; there can be up to a four-hour delay; deliveries are usually made twice a day (they had noticed that if there were more frequent deliveries, the folders would just sit on customer service representative II's desk)

Check part numbers:

- CSR II (Jane or John) receives order folders twice a day
- Checks parts numbers on computer system—10 seconds per line (.16m)
- Attaches revisions—10 seconds per line (.16m)
- Assigns a part number—15 seconds per line (.25m)
- Provides price estimate/lead time—60 seconds per line (1m)
- Returns folders by foot to customer sales representative I every two hours (120m)
- Two-hour queue time

Assign delivery date:

- CSR I assigns a delivery date—30 seconds per line (.5m)
- Files hardcopy—90 seconds per order (1.5m)
- Hand-carries acknowledgment and all papers to customer service representative II upon completion
- One-hour queue time (60m)

Verify order:
- CSR II reviews all prices/delivery dates—15 seconds per line item (.25m)
- Delivers orders to sales mailroom twice a day
- Four-hour queue time (240m)

Sales mail sort:
- Debbie sorts each order—30 seconds per order (.5m)
- Delivers mail to central mail room twice a day
- Four-hour queue time (240m)

Central mail sort:
- Joe posts each order and sends all hardcopy orders to customer daily—30 seconds per order (.5m)
- Eight-hour queue time (480m)

Creating the Premiere Current-State Map

The team proceeded to draw the current-state map, as follows:

1. Draw the external (or internal) customer and supplier at the top of the page, and list their requirements. Here the customer includes Clubs Company, Aces Company, APEX, Inc., and domestic distributors (see Figure 26). The customer is also the supplier in this case. If the customer and supplier were separate, an icon for each would be drawn at the top right and top left of the sheet, respectively.

Clubs, Aces, APEX Domestic Dist.

Orders processed within 1 day

Figure 26. Step 1 of Current-State Map

2. Draw the entry and exit processes to the value stream. In this case the team draws process boxes for the central mail sort at the far right portion of the page and to the far left portion of the map (see Figure 27).

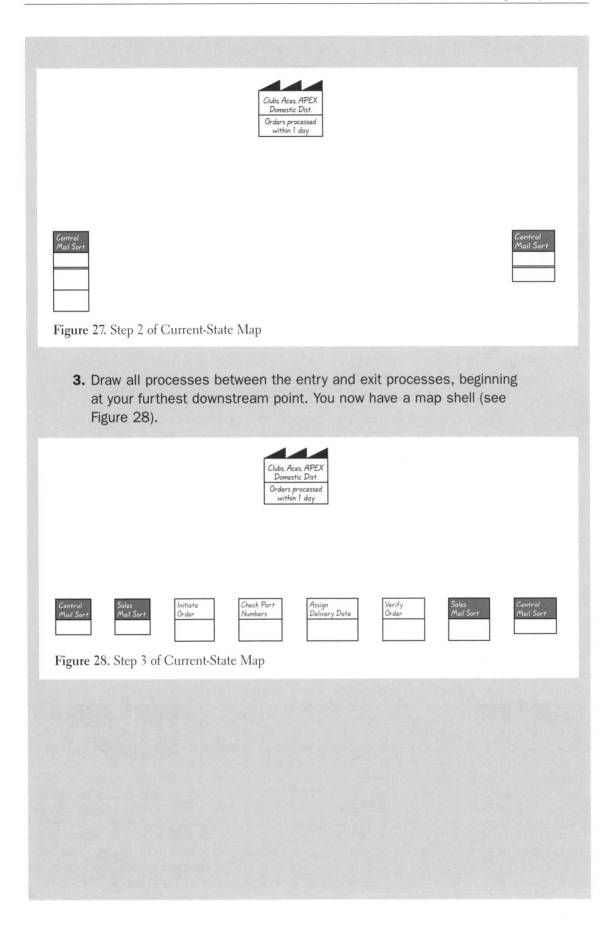

Figure 27. Step 2 of Current-State Map

3. Draw all processes between the entry and exit processes, beginning at your furthest downstream point. You now have a map shell (see Figure 28).

Figure 28. Step 3 of Current-State Map

4. List all process attributes (see Figure 29).

Figure 29. Step 4 of Current-State Map

5. Draw queue times between processes. Determine the queue time for an order to be entered. For example, since the mailroom only delivers once a day at 9:00 a.m., the queue time would run to the next day (i.e., queue time eight-hour work day). Be sure to use the same unit of measurement for all queue times—either hours or days (see Figure 30).

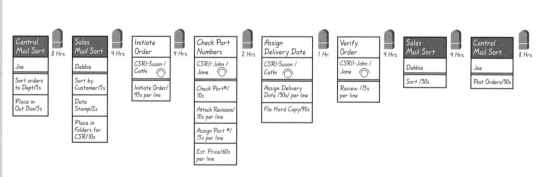

Figure 30. Step 5 of Current-State Map

6. Draw all communications that occur within the value stream (see Figure 31).

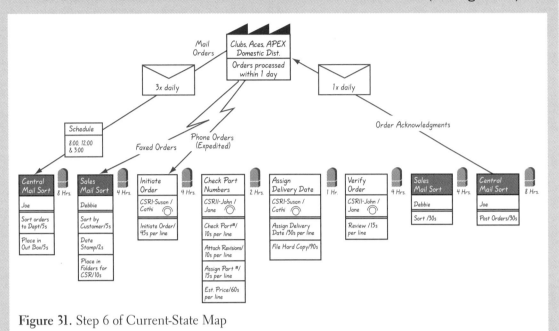

Figure 31. Step 6 of Current-State Map

7. Draw push or pull icons to identify the type of work flow (see Figure 32).

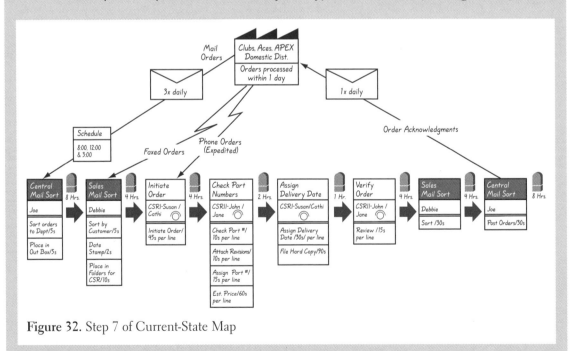

Figure 32. Step 7 of Current-State Map

8. Complete the map with any other data (see Figure 33). Determine the exceptions to the process areas and place them in the activity box, identified by an X. It is important to note the disruptions that impact the value stream. We will revisit these in the future state.

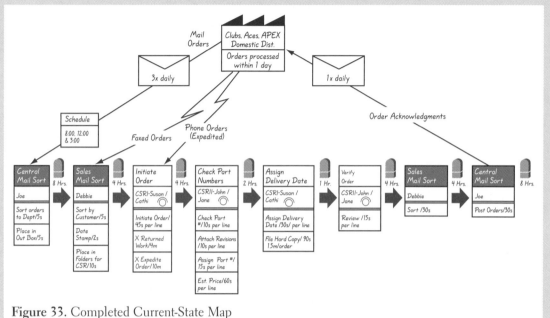

Figure 33. Completed Current-State Map

Step 4 Wrap-up

When the members of the core team have agreed that all the data recorded on the map is correct, create a clean, easy-to-read copy, date it, and post it on the VSM storyboard so it is visual in the workplace.

When drawing your completed map, keep in mind that many value streams have multiple lines that can merge and become confusing. Regardless of the complexity of the overall process, the objective is always the same: post enough detail to show how the value stream functions, but not so much that the map is confusing to read.

Keys to Successful Implementation

Because current-state mapping will prove so critical in efforts to evaluate the value stream you have chosen, to select appropriate metrics, and when mapping the future state, be sure to do a careful, thorough job. Here are some tips you will find helpful:

- You must understand where you are before you can decide where to go—so don't rush through this step.
- Draw on a white board or with pencil on a flipchart—you are bound to make many changes.
- Gather actual information—don't use "standard" data. For example, you may want to use a stopwatch to determine true cycle time.
- Focus on the most accurate and useful information.
- Reach a good balance between detail and clarity—if you need more detail you can create maps of smaller areas later.
- Think in terms of "flow." Observe how work units and information move upstream and downstream.
- Draw using icons.
- Take your time—do it right the first time!

You will encounter exceptions to processes. When you do, you may wish to show them on the map by marking an X in the attribute field for those processes. The team needs to understand the possible disruptions, what each process step is doing, and the potential frequency of exceptions.

There is always the rush toward improvement—a tendency to hurry through this step. Unfortunately, many future-state attempts for sustained implementation have failed precisely due to the desire to rush through current-state mapping. In these attempts, core team members did not spend the necessary time to collect actual or accurate data on the current state. *The foundation on which to build the future state must rest on solid data.*

Step 5. Identify Lean Metrics

Now that you have documented the current state, you are ready to determine the metrics that will best help you achieve your lean goals. The best way to get people to contribute to lean initiatives is to give them a simple means of understanding the impact of their efforts as they plan improvement activities, implement them, check the results, and make appropriate adjustments. Lean metrics provide such a means, thus helping to drive continuous improvement and waste elimination.

Lean Metrics: The Fundamentals

The goal of the *lean office* is to provide customers with what they want, when they want it, at a price they are willing to pay. Some standard lean measurables are:

- Project completion milestones
- Total work lead time
- Total work cycle time
- Internal errors
- Overtime
- Work load backlog

Lean Measurables and Waste

Lean measurables are always based on the seven deadly wastes. While some measurables are generic for nearly all value streams, there will be others that are specific to your particular value stream. Determining these depends a great deal on the specific circumstances of your value stream. The team charter, created during Step 1, will guide you in determining the measurables appropriate for your project because it provides strategic goals for the overall business. Your job in Step 5 is to identify the measurables from your value stream that support those strategic goals. After determining the relevant lean metrics, you may need to revise the charter.

Lean Measurables and Stratification

We begin by determining a few measurables that will drive waste elimination for the entire value stream. Then, as we dive deeper into the value stream, we can break those measurables into smaller pieces, or "stratify" them.

For example, the implementation team may study a value stream that services order fulfillment for one primary customer with the goal of achieving 100 percent on-time and accurate service. To meet this goal, the team may choose these three primary measurables:

1. Total order cycle time

2. Order-entry on-time delivery

3. Total number of errors

A measurable such as total order cycle time can be broken into many different pieces, such as:

- Time spent waiting
- Time spent walking
- Entering data
- Retrieving files
- Opening mail
- Processing time

An effective lean measurable is one that not only drives a value stream to improvement, but one that can be stratified into components, with each component addressing a specific waste in the system.

Don't Forget the Shopfloor

In choosing measurables for a VSM project, don't forget the impact that administrative or office improvements may have on shopfloor activities. Too often, administrative teams focus only on reduction of waste within the office and forget that they can also help reduce waste in the plant by streamlining procedures and improving standards that are connected to the typical manufacturing environment.

Setup Time Reduction through
Administrative Value Stream Management

One plant reported that their engineering office required a tooling report for each machine setup to be filed. This tooling report listed all the tooling used for the specific setup, the date, time, and setup operator.

In addition, each setup operator received an instruction form from his or her process router, with identical information on it, to be filled out as well.

Each report took on average two minutes to complete and file. There were about 10 filed each day. The elimination of this redundancy in the procedures saved nearly 100 hours of valuable operator time each year.

Steps for Application

Everyone on the core implementation team must first understand the purpose and importance of measurables. Then, to apply Step 5, they will perform the following activities:

1. Review the team charter for strategic direction.

2. Perform a lean office assessment in the value stream.

3. Determine lean measurables for management of the value stream.

4. Get management buy-in for the measurables (use catchball).

5. Calculate baseline measures.

6. Make the measures visual.

Lean Office Assessment

The lean office assessment is designed to be a self-evaluation. It is used to identify specific areas within the value stream upon which improvement initiatives can be focused (see Figure 34). Starting at the center, areas are shaded in to show the current state. White areas show where and how much improvement is needed.

This assessment also allows you to set a baseline and perform a "gap" analysis to compare your current state to a lean future state. It allows everyone at your site to discern at a glance where you are and where you hope to be when you achieve a more lean state.

The assessment is meant to monitor progress in relation to lean concepts and tools, and it will allow your teams to communicate lean language with a common visual tool. It is not meant to replace bottom-line measurables such as project completion percentage, value-added time, total cycle time, total workflow lead time and the like. An example page from the lean office assessment is shown in Figure 35 on page 73. (A complete assessment is included on the CD-ROM.)

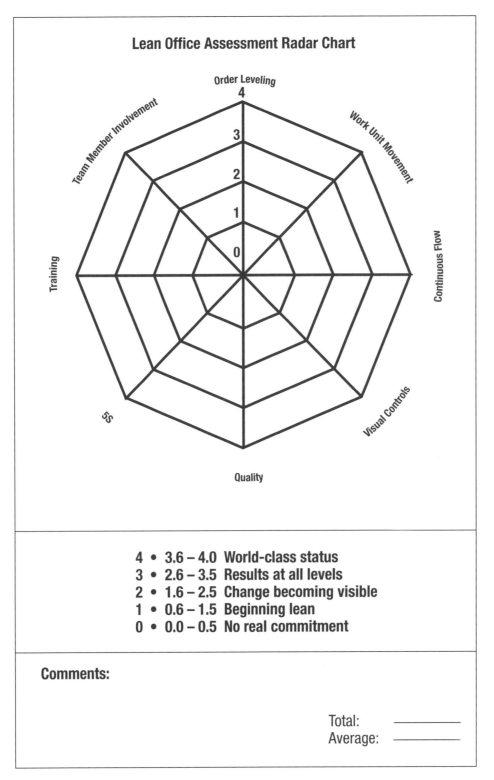

Figure 34. Lean Office Assessment Radar Chart

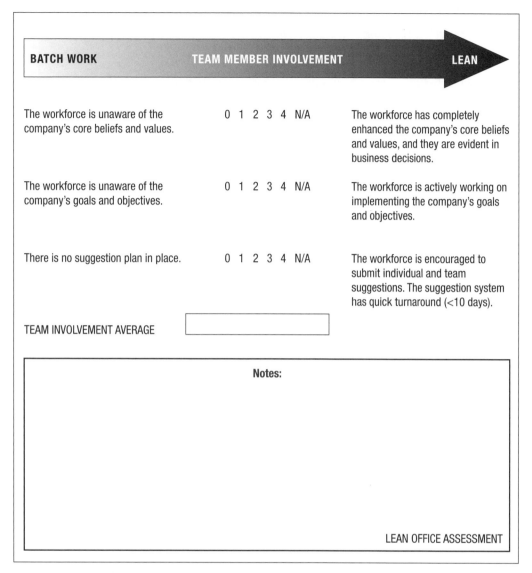

Figure 35. Example Page from Lean Office Assessment

Keys to Successful Implementation

For measurables to fulfill their purpose as drivers and motivators toward improvement, a few key principles must be kept in mind.

Continue to Play Catchball

As soon as the core implementation team has decided on lean measurables they should get management buy-in. In addition, they should get feedback from extended team members as well. In the future these extended team members will have to live by these measurables, so buy-in is crucial.

Standardize Measurements

How you measure something is as important as what you measure. To standardize measurements requires you to answer two crucial questions:

1. How can you make sure the results of the calculation are accurate and consistent?

2. How can you make sure that each measurement task is absolutely clear?

Just-in-Time Information

As you standardize your metrics you may want to use the principle of *just-in-time information*.

Just-in-time information is the right information, in the right form, in the hands of the people who need it, available when it is needed.

Measurables Should Be Easy to Collect

Measurables should be easy to understand and collect. Here are some guidelines for identifying and using lean measurables:

- Involve those responsible for implementing change in the creation of the data-gathering systems.
- Collect and review data when it is needed.
- Gather data where it is most useful.
- Make data accessible to the people who need it.
- Understand your "audience" before you report data.
- Ensure that the people who can make things happen get timely feedback.
- Ensure that data can be easily collected.

As you review performance progress, do not ignore small savings or improvements. Small improvements add up and are a key to the overall large gains of a lean implementation.

Make Measurables Visual

Always remember that measurables do one thing only: they provide information. If that information isn't shared, though, it becomes useless. Sharing measurables in a usable way not only makes them effective; it makes them the glue that holds the entire value stream management project together.

Imagine a basketball game without a score, without a scoreboard, and without a time clock. It would soon break down into chaos and "fooling around." It certainly wouldn't be interesting. Imagine a job so mindless that all the worker is asked to do is walk in a straight line, without any idea of how far he has gone or what he has accomplished. Why should we expect improvement?

Improvement occurs when people are interested and engaged in what is happening. Visual measurables, when done correctly, will accomplish this beyond your wildest expectations (see Figure 36).

Graphs are probably the most effective method available. A graph is easy to understand. It communicates more effectively than numbers or words alone. You can tell whether something is rising or falling. And graphs create an emotional reaction. When performance worsens, people want to do something about it. When it improves, they feel rewarded. No one has to tell them—the facts are there for all to see.

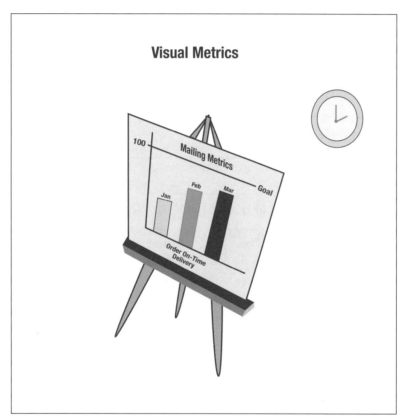

Figure 36. Visual Metrics

You've often heard the phrase, "Measurement is a process." That's because it's not something you perform once; it's ongoing and it involves all levels of an organization. And the measurables themselves may need to be refined as you learn more. But one thing is certain: without measurement you will never achieve continuous improvement and standardization.

Value stream mapping provides a very specific way to make measurements visual—by drawing a step chart of cycle and lead times at the bottom of the map. This visual display not only provides an understanding of total lead time, but also shows individual cycle and lead times and where they exist within the big picture (see Figure 37).

Cycle Time, Queue Time, and Lead time

Cycle time   is the time that elapses from the beginning of a process or individual activity until it is completed. Numerous cycle times may be included within an individual process or function. Cycle times are typically measured in minutes or seconds.

Total cycle time   is the sum of the cycle times for all the individual processes in a value stream. This is also referred to as *value-added time,* or VAT, because this is the time during which value should be added as the work unit flows through the process.

Queue time   is the time that a work unit will wait for a down-stream process to be ready to work on it.

Total lead time   is the total of all cycle times from all individual processes within the lean office value stream, plus the queue times that exist between each process.

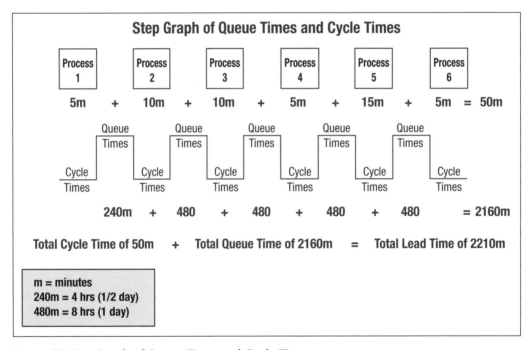

Figure 37. Step Graph of Queue Times and Cycle Times

Now, let's return to Premiere Manufacturing to see how they handled Step 5.

PREMIERE CASE STUDY—STEP 5

After reviewing the list of lean attributes and the current state, Premiere's core implementation team decides on the measurables that will work best for tracking progress toward the targets:

- Total cycle time and queue time—orders
- Total lead time—orders
- Percentage of orders entered within an eight-hour period
- Number of mistakes per million (work unit mistakes)
- Office lean assessment rating—quarterly

Total Order Cycle Time and Queue Time

The team determined the total order cycle time by looking at the current-state map. They made a list of the cycle times for each process the order passed through based on their average order of 15 line items. They converted all time units to minutes, dividing number of seconds by 60. The team then totaled the individual cycle times (see Figure 38).

Premiere's Total Order Cycle Time

.16m + .28m + 11.25m + 23.75m + 9m + 3.75m + .5m + .5m = 49.19

Central Mail Sort	Sales Mail Sort	Initiate Order	Check Part Nos.	Assign Delivery Date	Verify Order	Sales Mail Sort	Central Mail Sort
.16m	.28m	11.25m	23.75m	9m	3.75m	.5m	.5m

Figure 38. Premiere's Total Order Cycle Time

The team determined that total order cycle time is 49.19 minutes.

The team then listed the queue times for each process and totaled the queue times for the value stream (see Figure 39).

Premiere's Total Order Queue Time

480m + 240m + 240m + 120m + 60m + 240m + 240m + 480m = 2100m

Central Mail Sort	Sales Mail Sort	Initiate Order	Check Part Nos.	Assign Delivery Date	Verify Order	Sales Mail Sort	Central Mail Sort
480m	240m	240m	120m	60m	240m	240m	480m

Figure 39. Premiere's Total Order Queue Time

Total Order Lead Time

Cycle time may be interesting to managers, but lead time is interesting to customers. Lead time measures how long it takes for something to occur, from the perspective of the external customer. It is a true measure of service. To determine total order lead time, the team added the total cycle time to the total queue time.

The lead time is 2,149.19 minutes (add total cycle time + total queue time)
49.19 + 2,100 = 2,149.19

To determine the total lead time in hours, the team divided lead time by 60.

Lead time minutes/60 minutes per hour
2,149.19/60 = 35.82 hours

To determine the total lead time in workdays, the team divided lead time in hours by eight.

Lead time hours/8 hours per workday
35.82/8 = 4.48 workdays

Then they calculated the value added percentage—the total cycle time divided by the total lead time.

49.19/2149.19 = 2.3%

Only 2.3 percent of the total lead time for processing an order is spent on value-adding activities!

On-Time Delivery—Sales Orders Entered Within Eight Hours

This is an important customer service measurable because it is part of a larger, more important one—shipment within 24 hours of receipt of a customer order. Unfortunately, the team's research shows that they are performing at only 32 percent!

Defective Parts (or Work) per Million (DPPM)

This is the team's quality measurable. It measures the actual number of line items with mistakes made on an order or quote. For example, if two line items are wrong on the same order, that would measure as two mistakes. Each line item entry counts as an opportunity for error. Their research showed that for the past four weeks they had 38 errors (wrong customer ID, wrong discount, part number incorrectly entered, date missing, etc.). To calculate DPPM, you would divide total errors by total opportunities for errors of 8,100 line items and multiply by 1,000,000. Therefore, the DPPM is $38/8{,}100 \times 1{,}000{,}000$, which is 4,691 DPPM.

Office Lean Assessment Rating—Quarterly

Premiere's core implementation team completed the assessment at one of their weekly meetings. Their scores are shown as shaded areas in Figure 40.

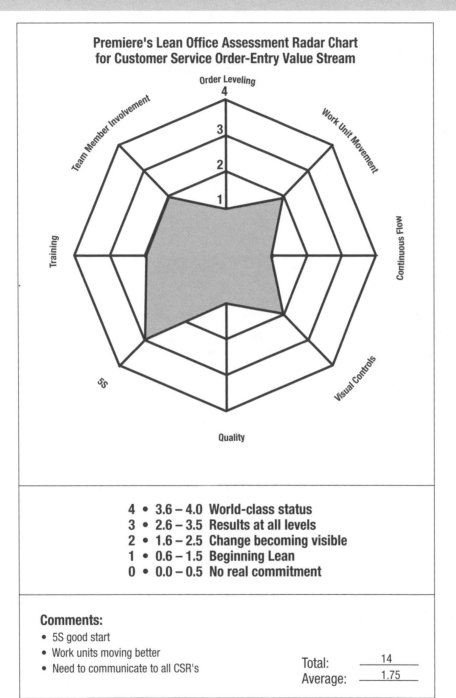

Premiere's Lean Office Assessment Radar Chart for Customer Service Order-Entry Value Stream

4 • 3.6 – 4.0 **World-class status**
3 • 2.6 – 3.5 **Results at all levels**
2 • 1.6 – 2.5 **Change becoming visible**
1 • 0.6 – 1.5 **Beginning Lean**
0 • 0.0 – 0.5 **No real commitment**

Comments:
• 5S good start
• Work units moving better
• Need to communicate to all CSR's

Total: _____14_____
Average: _____1.75_____

Figure 40. Premiere's Current-State Lean Office Assessment

After completing the assessment, they finalized their decision about appropriate lean measurables to direct them toward their improvement efforts. Figure 41 lists the Premiere measurables and the baseline measures. The targets for a six-month period will be added in Step 7.

Lean Measurable	Baseline Measure	Target (six months)
Total order cycle time	49.19 minutes	
Total order lead time	4.5 days	
On-time delivery (% orders entered during 8-hour period)	32%	
Number of defective parts per million	4691 DPPM	
Lean assessment	14	

Figure 41. Lean Measurables, Baseline Measures

Cycle and Lead-Time Step Charts

Before moving on to Step 6 one more task remains. The team returns to the current-state map and posts the baseline data for cycle and lead times in the form of a step chart, at the bottom of the map (see Figure 42). They post the updated map and baseline metrics on the storyboard.

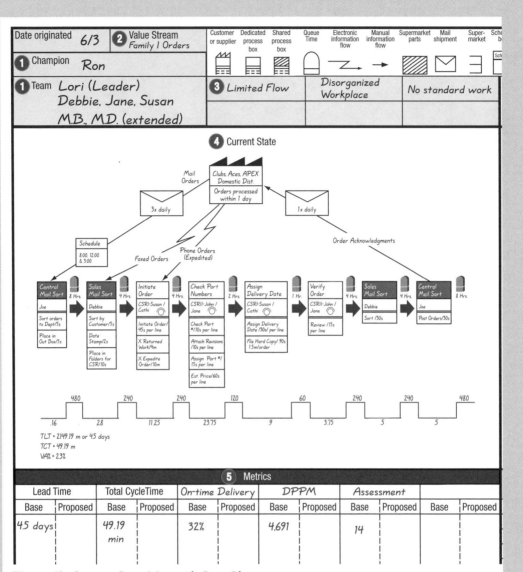

Figure 42. Current-State Map with Step Charts

Step 6–Phase I. Map the Future State— Customer Demand

At this point the core implementation team has mapped the current state, performed a lean office assessment, and chosen lean measurables for the value stream. They have learned how to see and think lean. Now it is time to tap the creativity of the workforce and the core implementation team to design the future state. An understanding of how lean applies to administrative value streams is never more crucial than in Step 6. Mapping the future state of a value stream involves identifying all the administrative lean tools—such as FIFO lanes, work-area design, supermarkets, and 5S—that will help ensure you can meet customer requirements, establish a continuous workflow, and distribute work evenly. Your future-state map will actually show where these tools are to be used.

The process for mapping the future state takes place in three phases:

1. Customer demand phase. Understand the customer demand for your services and work units, including quality characteristics and lead time.

2. Continuous flow phase. Implement continuous flow so that internal and external customers receive the right work unit, at the right time, in the right quantity.

3. Leveling phase. Distribute work evenly, by volume and variety, to reduce queue times and allow smaller work units to move, if practical.

In this first section of Step 6 we will be focusing on the customer demand phase of the future state. We will describe the techniques associated with determining customer demand, the tools that can be used to meet it, and the process for mapping.

Phase I: Customer Demand

How often have you heard the statement "The customer is number one," but seen very little done to actually ensure customer satisfaction? By focusing on customer demand first you *will* do something about this. Your efforts in this phase will apply specific measures and techniques to ensure consistent fulfillment of customer requirements. You will:

1. Determine takt time.

2. Establish pitch.

3. Determine how to meet demand through:

    a. Buffer and safety resources

    b. 5S for the office

    c. Problem-solving methods

Questions for Focus on Demand

Application of the demand phase can be summarized by the following questions:

- What is the demand? In other words, what is the takt time?

- Are you overproducing, underproducing, or meeting demand?

- Can you meet takt time (or pitch) with current administrative capabilities?

- Do you need administrative buffer resources? Where?

- Do you need administrative safety resources? Where?

- What problems need to be solved *right now*?

- Where does your office need organization, ordering, and cleaning? To what degree?

Determine Takt Time

From the data you collect on customer demand, you will determine takt time.

Takt Time

Takt time is the pace of customer demand.

Takt is a German word for a musical beat or rhythm. Just as a metronome keeps a musical beat, takt time keeps the beat for customer demand. Takt determines how fast a process needs to run in order to meet customer demand. You must keep this rhythm of work flowing throughout the value stream to ensure that you can deliver what your customer has requested.

Takt Time Examples

- An engineering Type A drawing produced every two hours

- An order entered every five minutes

- An employment application filed every two days

- A quote returned to the customer every 60 minutes

To calculate takt time for a particular value stream, divide the daily net available operating time by the total quantity of work units required for one day. The net available operating time is the total available work time minus meetings, breaks, lunch, and any other non-value-adding activities. If a workday runs from 8:00 a.m. until 4:30 p.m. (510 minutes), with a 30-minute lunch and two 10-minute breaks, the net available operating work time is 460 minutes.

Takt Time Formula

Takt time = Net available operating time ÷ total daily quantity required

---

For example, the drafting department works from 8:00 a.m. to 5:00 p.m., with a one-hour lunch. The daily net available work time is eight hours. If you have determined that during the past three months the drafting department has produced 240 drawings for a particular customer, the total number of work items required per day is 240 divided by three months, or 80 per month. There are 20 workdays per month, so the daily work unit requirement is 80 divided by 20, or four drawings. The takt time calculation is:

Takt time = 8 hours ÷ 4 drawings = 2 hours per drawing

You may be asking yourself, what do drafting department drawings have to do with customers and customer demand? While it is true that this drafting department doesn't have a traditional money-paying customer, as a value stream it still has customers, and these customers have demands. The only difference between this case example and a traditional example is that here the customer is *inside* the company.

Determining administrative customer demand is not an exact science. You can use historical data, or the team can develop new data-collection techniques to determine the required work quantity. The key is to find a measurable unit of work with which you can associate a processing time. You will also need to choose an appropriate time period to use in analyzing demand data, one that is long enough to reflect typical variations in demand.

Examples of Customer Demand Data

- For phone-in orders, look at the number received for the last month.
- For job applications, look at the average number received for one year.
- For customer information inquiries, review the last three months.

Establish Pitch

Takt time is a useful tool, but office workers aren't robots. In many cases, you may not want to move work units through the value stream at the true takt time pace. For instance, it may not be practical in the drafting department example to move a drawing every two hours. In that case, you would use pitch to determine the optimal workflow quantity.

Pitch

Pitch is a multiple of takt time that will allow you to create, maintain, and sustain a consistent and practical workflow throughout the value stream. It establishes a workflow for a work unit to move from the beginning to the end of the value stream.

To calculate pitch, multiply the takt time by the number of work units to be grouped to flow through the system in a manageable way.

Pitch Formula

Pitch = takt time × number of work units

Pitch allows for a measurable, manageable amount of work to be released to the work area, establishing a pace. The flow of work should be continuous and smooth. If something disrupts this pace, then problems can be identified within the pitch time frame and corrected immediately. You will not have to wait until the end of the day to determine if you are on schedule. You will know within your pitch increment whether or not you are meeting customer demand.

In the drafting example given, the drafting department finds that engineering can respond to drawings twice a day. They decide to move two drawings to engineering every four hours, establishing a pitch of four hours.

In the customer service department, the considerations are different. Say the customer demand for order entry averages one order every five minutes. Because this is an average and the size and complexity of actual orders vary significantly, it is not practical to move work through the value stream every five minutes. It would be more realistic to have a pitch of two hours. This means moving orders in groups of 24 [five minutes per order × 24 = 120 minutes or two hours]. We generally recommend that you have a pitch of not less than two hours and not more than eight hours. Pitch will be the time element that will determine how often or when the work units, or group of work units, is moved throughout the value stream (see Figure 43).

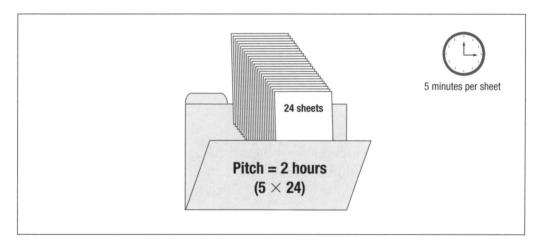

Figure 43. Work Unit with Pitch

Pitch helps create a sense of urgency—momentum for the lean office. Without it, everyone will produce to his or her own schedule, or what he or she thinks is required for that day. Ensuring that pitch is met is mandatory for the creation of a lean value stream.

Determine How to Meet Customer Demand

As soon as you have determined customer demand, you must make the commitment to meet it—*now.* You do not want to wait until the future state is completed, as that may take six months or more. If you cannot meet demand with your current processes, you can use lean tools such as buffer and safety resources.

Buffer and Safety Resources

Buffer and safety resources help ensure that customer demand is met under all conditions. The need for a tool such as a buffer resource arises in an administrative value stream because the volume of work required by the customer is not always exact. There may be wide variations in customer requirements. Buffer resources are used to provide a "buffer" against these variations in demand. They are allocated resources within the value stream to help meet takt time in these cases.

Buffer and Safety Resources	
Buffer resources	A means of meeting customer demand when customer ordering patterns, or takt times, vary.
Safety resources	A means of meeting customer demand when internal constraints or inefficiencies disrupt process flow.

A buffer resource has to work immediately when needed. It's not something that can be allowed to be bogged down in administrative scheduling or budgetary haggling. There is only one consideration for a buffer resource: when customer demand requires it, it is available! So it's important to have buffer resources ready or available ahead of a spike in demand to ensure that the demand is met.

Safety resources are needed to deal with internal workflow inefficiencies, which may be due to poor standards, insufficient training, shifts in priorities, lack of planning, and so forth. Safety resources are often identical to buffer resources. However, an additional way to provide safety resources is via a contingency plan.

Buffer and safety resources can include:

- Overtime
- Temporary workers
- Retirees
- Departmental borrowing

For example, if there are four people in the customer service department handling 100 orders a day and someone calls in sick, there are only three people to handle 100 orders. Here the safety resources would be a contingency plan to enable those three people to handle an additional 25 orders. It could consist of one or more of the following:

- Each customer service representative agreeing to work overtime.
- The department manager agreeing to spend two hours processing orders.
- The department administrative assistant receiving clearly defined instructions to assist with order processing.

Remember one thing: always plan and record your need for buffer and safety resources separately. You want to have clear data about the costs associated with fluctuating customer demand versus internal process problems. Also remember that buffer and safety resources are only temporary measures that allow you to meet customer demand while you are in transition to your future state. Continual improvement efforts should always target the reduction of buffer and safety resources.

The 5S System

How much time did you spend actually doing your job today? How much time was wasted searching for information, files, and whatnot? How much time was wasted walking to retrieve a printout, fax, file, or the like? How much paper is being wasted in your office? Are mistakes being made because you use inaccurate or outdated information?

The 5S System

5S is an improvement process, originally summarized by five Japanese words beginning with S, to create a workplace that will meet the criteria of visual control and lean.

The 5S system addresses all of these issues. In 5S you will organize and standardize your workplace step by step, and in the process reduce waste. It is the first improvement activity that the team will perform. As a result, the workers will regain control of the workplace (see Figures 44 and 45).

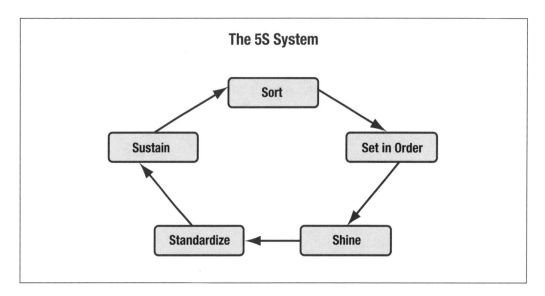

Figure 44. The 5S System

The 5S system consists of five activities:

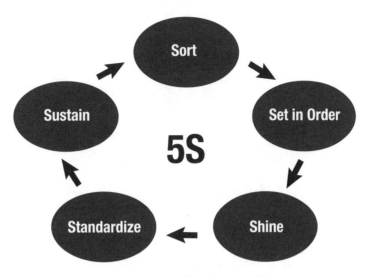

Figure 45. The 5S Circle of Accomplishments

1. *Sort* involves sorting through the contents of an area and removing unnecessary items such as files, supplies, tools, equipment, and books—including contents of drawers.

2. *Set-in-order* involves arranging necessary items for easy and efficient access, and keeping them that way. This includes individual workstations as well as team work areas, meeting areas, mailrooms, and storage rooms.

3. *Shine* involves cleaning everything, keeping it clean, and using cleaning as a way to ensure that your area and equipment are properly maintained.

4. *Standardize* involves creating guidelines for keeping the area organized, orderly, and clean, and making standards visual and obvious.

5. *Sustain* involves education and communication to ensure that everyone follows the 5S standards.

5S is sometimes seen as merely an organized housecleaning method, but it is much more than that. By implementing the 5S system you will reduce the time you spend on non-value-adding work by up to 25 percent—time that you can spend meeting customer demand. Many organizations find it helpful to visually post a "5S circle" and acknowledge each step completed with some sort of recognition (lunch for the team, a gift from the company catalog, etc.). (See Figure 46.)

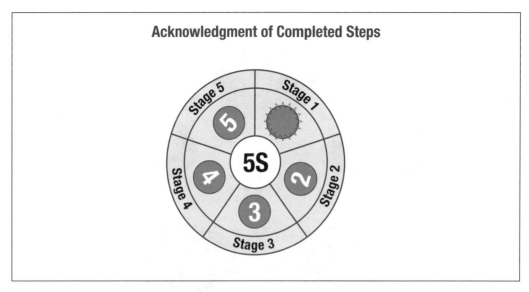

Figure 46. "5S Circle"—Acknowledgment of Completed Steps

Problem-Solving Model

In order to improve performance immediately and serve customer demand, teams will need to solve problems as a group. We're not referring to long-term, systemic problems, but rather the "low-hanging fruit" that can be addressed in the first two months of the project. But working together while trying to be creative *and* analytical can be confusing. Therefore, the team needs a model that will help it do both.

There are many problem-solving models available. However, most of them agree that it is the sequence of activities that is most important, and those activities must include:

- Defining the problem
- Analyzing possible causes
- Identifying possible solutions
- Developing an action plan
- Evaluating and renewing the action plan
- Standardizing effective ideas

Excellent companies have a healthy philosophy of problem solving, take the time to train teams in problem solving, and give their teams time to solve problems. These activities are especially helpful prior to mapping the customer demand phase of value stream management.

Preparing to Map the Future State

Before actually mapping the customer demand phase of the future state, there are a number of things you should do:

1. Determine the takt time and pitch (if appropriate).
2. Determine whether you are overproducing, underproducing, or meeting demand.
3. Review the current-state map. If any questions arise regarding the current state as you plan the future state, revisit the appropriate work areas for clarification.

We recommend that you map the future state on a flipchart using a pencil—or on a white board using dry-erase markers. Remember that you will show on the future-state map the areas where you have introduced the improvement tools we mentioned earlier, and that your map is bound to change as you progress and acquire more and better information. Be flexible with your future-state map. It is good to keep a separate copy of your map at this phase, before you add continuous flow elements to it.

How to Draw the Customer-Demand-Phase Map

Mapping the future state begins with the following steps:

1. Start the future-state map by drawing the customer and supplier (if different from the customer) in the same position(s) as you did on the current-state map—usually at the top of the page.
2. Fill in customer requirements, takt time, and pitch.
3. Place the *last* process at the right portion of the page. This is the most downstream process for satisfying the customer demand.
4. At the left portion of the page, place the upstream process that would initiate the customer request or demand. This is done to ensure you have your value stream boundaries set.
5. Draw communication between the customer (and supplier) and these processes.

You now have a map shell.

6. Determine how and when buffer and safety resources are needed, and draw those icons on the map. These may change later, after you have performed the next improvement phases.
7. Determine where 5S should be implemented, and draw a kaizen focus icon on the map in the appropriate places.

    Note: even though you may be constantly changing things and testing various lean methods, do not wait for everything to be completed to begin 5S. You can do at least the first three 5S activities.
8. Determine where problem-solving projects should be implemented to meet customer demand, and draw kaizen focus icons on the map.

At this point you are not changing the current-state process flow. That will occur in the next phase.

Figure 47 displays the new icons you will use to map the future state.

Demand-Phase Icons	
Purpose	**Icon**
Buffer Resources	B B
Safety Resources	S S
Kaizen Focus (Improvement activity)	
Cart	

Figure 47. Demand-Phase Icons

PREMIERE CASE STUDY—STEP 6–PHASE I

Premiere Manufacturing has decided to make a commitment to ensure that customer demand—takt time—is met. They chose order fulfillment as their focus.

Determine Takt Time

The total daily available work time is eight hours, or 480 minutes. In order to calculate the daily production requirements, the team needed a unit of measurement that could be standardized and associated with a cycle time. They decided to use the number of line items in each order. The team analyzed a spreadsheet with data for the prior 12 weeks to determine the total volume of order line items received from customers for that period. The total quantity of line items was 28,800.

The team then determined the average daily quantity of line items by determining the number of workdays in the period, then dividing the total number of line items by that number:

$$5 \text{ days per week} \times 12 \text{ weeks} = 60 \text{ days}$$
$$28,800 \text{ line items} \div 60 \text{ days} = 480 \text{ line items per day}$$

So the daily average work quantity received was 480 line items per day:

$$\text{Takt time} = 480 \text{ minutes} \div 480 \text{ line items}$$
Takt time = 1 minute per line item

This is the rate of customer demand.

The team decided that it needed to look at the total requirements for all types of work units for customer service, so it used the same method of data collection to determine the takt time for expedited orders and returned work units. Even though these activities were exceptions to the target value stream, the team thought it a good idea to include them to get a picture of overall customer service duties.

The team found that the work quantity for expedited orders was 10 orders per day. The takt time for expedited orders was 480 minutes divided by 10, or 48 minutes:

Takt time = 48 minutes per expedited order

The returned work unit requests were 11.25 per day, with a takt time of 480 divided by 11.25, or 42.67 minutes:

Takt time = 42.67 minutes per returned work unit request

Establish Pitch

In Step 4, the team had calculated that an average order is 15 line items:

Pitch = Takt time × number of work units
Pitch = 1 minute × 15 line items per order = 15 minutes per order

The team thought it would be unrealistic to move one order at a time through the value stream. They looked for a period of time that would break up the day, so that they could monitor whether they were keeping up with demand and could pull in extra resources if needed. They also reviewed the mail delivery schedule (three times daily) and concluded that they would start with a two-hour pitch, which would allow them to move orders in groups of eight (see Figure 48).

Pitch = 8 orders × 15 minutes = 2 hours

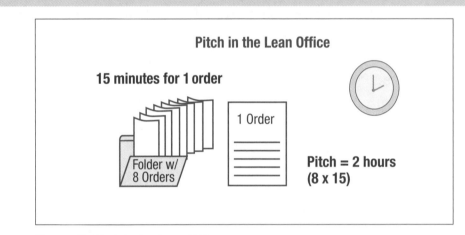

Figure 48. Pitch in the Lean Office

Determine How to Meet Demand

Premiere's team realized they could not consistently meet customer demand and had to correct a number of problems in the demand phase of Step 6. The survey data had shown that they were meeting the one-day turnaround time only 32 percent of the time. They began by drawing a future-state map for the demand phase.

Drawing the Map

They began drawing the map by forming an outer shell, just as they did when they created the current-state map. They drew the icon for the customer, the first and last processes, and communications between those processes and the customer. They added the customer requirements, including takt time and pitch (see Figure 49).

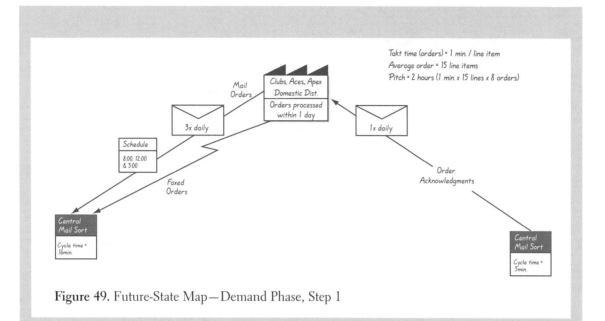

Figure 49. Future-State Map—Demand Phase, Step 1

The team reviewed the mailroom processes to determine optimal use of mailroom personnel to eliminate or reduce queue time. They decided to have the mail delivered from the central mailroom three times daily (instead of once), and to use a mailroom person to deliver the mail and faxes directly to the customer service supervisor on a cart. This eliminated the need for the mail to go through the sales mailroom. Phone orders would come in directly to the customer service supervisor.

To indicate this design decision, the team drew icons of a mail cart and the customer service supervisor on the map, after the central mailroom (see Figure 50).

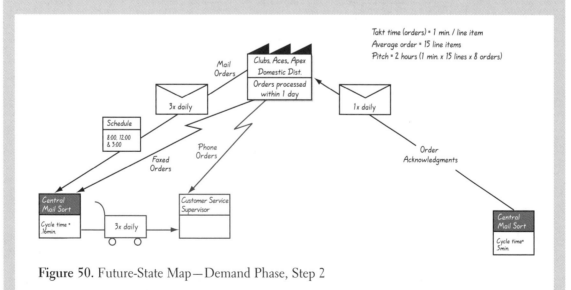

Figure 50. Future-State Map—Demand Phase, Step 2

Buffer and Safety Resources

The team realized that by measuring the pitch of eight orders per two hours and delivering mail and faxes to the customer service supervisor three times each day, they could more easily predict when they were behind in their orders. They devised a buffer and safety resource plan that relied on four strategies to immediately fill customer orders:

Strategy 1: Teamwork. When one team member is behind, others help.

Strategy 2: Supervisor. If teamwork is not enough, the supervisor fills orders until the team catches up.

Strategy 3: Overtime. By the end of the day, if there are any lagging orders, the supervisor can authorize overtime.

Strategy 4: Temps. If necessary, the supervisor can authorize the hiring of temps (the next day) to catch up on orders.

After deciding the strategies, the team drew buffer and safety icons on the map where the orders enter the system, immediately after the customer service supervisor (see Figure 51).

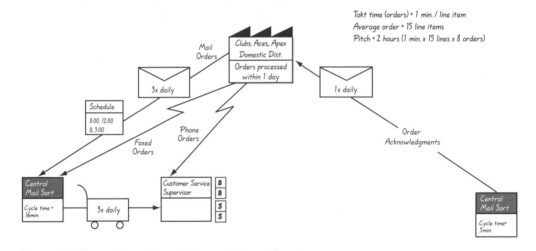

Figure 51. Future-State Map—Demand Phase, Step 3

Improvement Methods

The team determined that the following improvement methods would help them consistently meet demand.

Implementing 5S

The team decided that 5S would be implemented throughout the target area covered by the value stream, and that it would be the first improvement activity to occur. They realized that a major issue in 5S was management of office supplies and equipment.

Problem-Solving Projects

The team realized that even though, in the long run, the entire process would be redesigned, there were many problems that needed solving immediately. They identified two projects that would need to be implemented almost immediately:

- Mail cart design
- Buffer and safety resource implementation process/communication

The team drew kaizen icons on the map to indicate these improvement methods. This completed their demand-phase map (see Figure 52).

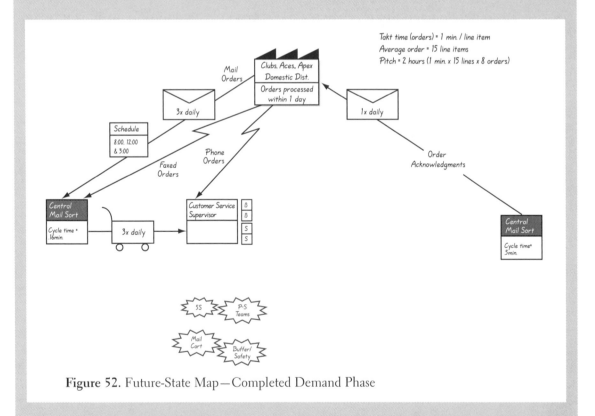

Figure 52. Future-State Map—Completed Demand Phase

Keys to Successful Implementation

In order to implement the demand phase successfully, the core implementation team must:

1. Understand customer demand.

You must spend the time upfront to understand customer demand thoroughly. It is the foundation upon which your lean system will be built. If your customer is another functional area, you must work with them until you know their requirements. Collecting accurate data is important. Determining customer demand for administration may be difficult, but it can be done.

2. Don't attempt to microdesign the future state at this phase.

You will not need to identify specific action items to implement this phase of the future state. That will come in Step 7. The intent here is to create the overall future state and fill in the details later. You are still in the design, not the testing, phase.

3. Be flexible.

Tracking customer demand in the office may require constant adjustments in your plans for the future state. Be flexible. Do not hold too tightly to any one set of ideas. Instead, think of ideas as being in a process of evolution. As people learn and grow, they will take more responsibility and make better decisions.

4. Create a plan that the whole team can agree on.

One of the best ways to make sure a plan will work is to get rapid buy-in. The team should follow these few guidelines to make sure they agree on the plan:

- Restate the original problem and review the current-state map.
- Review the metrics.
- Review the takt and pitch times.
- Review all ideas posted on the customer demand-phase map, as well as others discussed but not posted—and the reasons why.
- Review problem-solving projects listed.
- Make final changes.
- Get buy-in from everyone.
- Post the map on the storyboard and update it as progress is made. Put it in a common area along with the team charter.

Step 6–Phase II. Map the Future State— Continuous Flow

In the previous chapter, "Map the Future State—Customer Demand," you began to develop a lean future state by drawing a value stream map to meet customer demand. In this section, you will continue this process to enable you to create continuous flow, assuring that internal and external customers receive the right work unit, at the right time, in the right quantity. We will describe the techniques associated with continuous flow and the process for mapping a future state that incorporates continuous flow methods. In this phase you will apply specific measures and techniques to ensure consistent fulfillment of customer requirements. You will:

1. Develop a *continuous flow* point of view.

2. Decide how to *control the flow of work* throughout the value stream.

3. Perform *line balancing* for the target value stream.

4. Implement *standardized work* for all processes.

5. Determine the *layout* of the work area.

Questions for Focus on Continuous Flow

Application of the continuous flow phase can be summarized by the following questions:

- Where can you apply continuous flow?
- What level of flow do you need?
  - One work unit?
  - Small lots of work units?
- What type and shape of cell design will you use?
- How will you control upstream work?
- Will you use kanban?
- Will you have in-process supermarkets?
- Will you apply FIFO?
- What other improvement methods will help to achieve continuous flow?

Understanding Continuous Flow

At the heart of lean is just-in-time production, or continuous flow.

Continuous Flow

Continuous flow means producing work according to three key principles:

- Only what is needed

- Just when it is needed

- In the exact amount needed

Pull

The ideal state of continuous flow is characterized by the ability to replenish a single work unit when the customer has pulled it. It can be summarized in the simple statement: "Move one, make one." In the office the concept is slightly different because you don't always have a customer "pulling" a piece for you to replace. You must understand precisely what a downstream process requires in order to ensure that when they need the upstream work unit, it is available—no later, no sooner. This often may be a certain segment of the work unit. In our HR example, it may be certain qualified applicants on a pre-approved list, which the HR assistant keeps up to date and available at the demand of the downstream customer—the HR manager.

In administration, continuous flow is characterized by the ability to perform only the work that is needed at the moment, no more and no less. Furthermore, it means that you are never behind and that if there isn't enough work for you to do, the system balances itself so that everyone has equal work. The important point is to banish waste in all its forms. You do not want to create any work (or work units) that is not required from the downstream process (or customer). How many times are reports or data generated, or meetings held, that have no real purpose and add no value to the end customer? Utilizing this concept and its tools will eliminate this type of waste.

"Impossible!," you might say. But the goal of administrative continuous flow has in fact been achieved, but *only* through a major change in perspective. Instead of worrying about the needs and efficiency of a single operation, we have to prioritize the needs of the entire process. Put another way, we look at the overall workflow instead of taking a static picture of one work area or one person's duties (see Figure 53).

Seamless continuous flow requires that the customer demand tools—takt time, pitch, buffer and safety resources, and 5S—must already be in effect so that you can work on flow without interrupting the delivery of work to your customer. We also highly recommend that you implement problem-solving teams to address the many physical and psychological barriers to change.

Having gained a flow perspective, you are now ready to control the work.

> ### *Advantages of Continuous Flow Processes*
>
> - Shorter lead times
> - Drastic reduction of work-in-process (and piles of paper on desks)
> - Drastic reduction of queue times
> - Ability to identify problems and fix them earlier
> - Reduced work unit and paper conveyance
> - Reduced paper handling, and number of people handling
> - Flexibility in meeting changes in customer demand (takt time)
> - Easier detection of problems
> - Less worker frustration

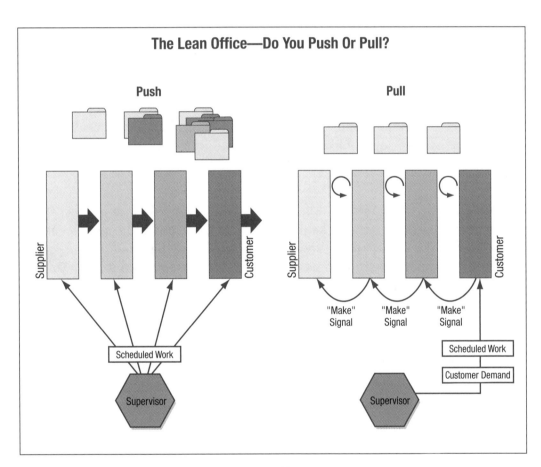

Figure 53. The Lean Office—Do You Push or Pull?

Control the Flow of Work

Have you ever gone behind the scenes into the storage area of a first-rate supermarket? If it's a truly well run supermarket, the answer would be "no"—because supermarkets don't typically have storage for many of their goods. Every item is received and transferred straight to the shelves, where it is available to the customer. No costly storage. No large storage areas. No waiting. The goods are always fresh.

The supermarket holds the goods between you (the customer) and the various vendors supplying the store. It is required to do so due to variations in customer demand. The customer's lead time needs to be minimal: i.e., the time to select something off a shelf. It would not be feasible for the supplier or vendor to have just one item there. An ordering pattern needs to be established. Therefore, minimum and maximum levels are set so that a balance exists between what the customer wants, and when, and the frequency of deliveries to the store.

This is called a *pull* system. Only the amount that has been used by the customer, or "pulled," is reordered. The maximum standard is never exceeded. Studying purchasing patterns and making seasonal adjustments gives management a good idea of how much to keep on the shelf at any given time.

This holds true for your administrative processes. You must first understand what is required downstream and organize the work upstream to support those requirements. (This will be further demonstrated in the Premiere case study.)

Another way to control the workflow between processes is the first in, first out (FIFO) method. One of the best demonstrations of FIFO is in the dairy section of a supermarket. Facing the customer is a downward tilted shelf holding milk cartons. The cartons are stacked from the back by supermarket workers several times each day. The first to be delivered are the first to be stacked, and therefore the first to be purchased by the customer. It's automatic because of the FIFO design.

Well-run supermarkets have one more feature that controls the flow of product throughout their system—a reorder card (or kanban). Somewhere close to the shelf location, usually on the front, is all the information needed to reorder that product. No searching. No misfiling. No wondering. In lean we call this system *kanban*, and it has revolutionized the way we manage inventory. Supermarket pull, kanban, and FIFO all have tremendous potential to control the flow of work in our offices and save thousands of hours of work time. Let's see how these tools apply to administrative lean.

In-Process Supermarkets

Where obstacles to continuous flow—moving one work unit at a time—exist, you can use a supermarket system. A supermarket of work-in-process may be necessary to ensure that flow is possible. It is used when cycle time variations between processes exist.

Supermarket

A system used to store a set level of completed work units or partially completed work units (WIP) and replenish what is "pulled" to fulfill customer orders (internal and external). A supermarket is used when circumstances make it difficult to sustain continuous flow.

Let's say your personnel department is consistently behind in scheduling interviews to respond to good applicants. They may be receiving too many applications, or it may be that the HR manager cannot easily locate the list of potential applicants. By the time a potential applicant is contacted, that person is no longer interested. In any event, the flow of applications needs to be addressed.

Establishing a supermarket between the HR assistant and the HR manager could improve the flow. The assistant could set up folders that are color-coded by job classification. Each would have a certain number of applications for the manager to review. When one folder was removed, it would be replaced with another. The empty folder would be sent back to the assistant as a signal to replenish. This would be the kanban.

Toyota found the supermarket to be the best alternative to scheduling upstream processes that cannot flow continuously. As you improve flow, the need for supermarkets may decrease. Remember that supermarkets are a compromise to the ideal state, as with pitch and buffer and safety resources. You will not achieve your ideal state overnight, but you must continually work towards that ideal state.

The Kanban System

The kanban system was created in lean manufacturing to manage the flow of work units in and out of supermarkets and work areas. It is a unique way to deliver the required amount of an essential work unit exactly when it is needed. Kanban is a form of visual control, using cards to trigger action and reorder. The successful implementation of a kanban system will make it possible to cut queue time by to up to 50 percent or more (see Figure 54).

> ### The Origin of Kanban
>
> In Japanese, *kanban* means "card," billboard," or "sign." Kanban refers to the inventory control card used in a pull system. Kanban also is used synonymously to refer to the inventory control system developed for use within the Toyota Production System.

Kanban can be transferred directly from factory to office use in management of inventory, supplies, and small equipment. But the true power of kanban in administration is its use to signal actions or events, and the details of that action or event.

Basics of Kanban

Kanban applies a form of visual control (information that can be understood by anyone) to the movement of work units. This information states when, who, what, and how many—essentially all information needed for movement.

Kanban for the administrative area can be anything from an actual index card for ordering supplies to a folder that has work within it. There needs to be a mailbox, a device for the folder to be deposited into after use, and a visual board, or file for organizing the kanban (to be discussed further in the leveling phase of this step).

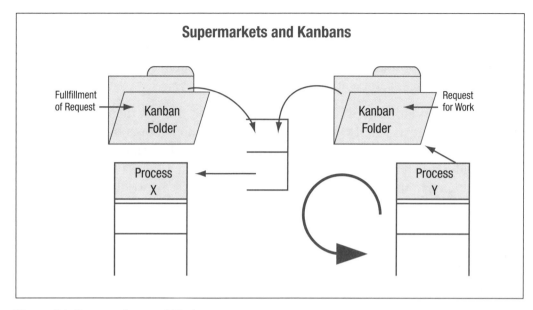

Figure 54. Supermarkets and Kanbans

First In, First Out (FIFO)

In administrative processes each job—every order, invoice, or request for a quote—is likely to be different. Every engineering design is unique. Every budget is different. And they usually have time requirements placed on them. For that reason, FIFO is a good practice to follow. Simply put, every job should be processed in the order that it enters the process, through FIFO.

FIFO is more than a rule. In implementing FIFO you must make it physically difficult, if not impossible, to draw and work on anything other than the earliest (oldest) work (or jobs) first.

> ### FIFO
> First in, first out (FIFO) is a work-control method used to ensure that the oldest work (first in) is the first to be processed (first out).

A FIFO *lane*:

1. Holds a designated amount of work (or jobs) between two operations.
2. Is sequentially loaded.
3. Uses a signal to notify the upstream operation to stop loading when the lane is full (to prevent overloading) and has a process in place to react.
4. Requires rules and procedures for upstream and downstream operations.
5. Uses visual displays and controls to ensure adherence to rules and procedures.
6. Requires discipline by the workforce to ensure FIFO integrity: When the FIFO lane is full, the upstream process should produce no more work! The signal used to con-

vey this can be verbal, visual, or a priority email request. Urgency in responding to these cues will assure the integrity of the process.

FIFO can be used alone or in conjunction with other tools such as work area design and in-process supermarkets. For example, in the customer service area, to control the flow of orders, the FIFO lane can include a certain quantity of orders that move through the order entry process, and a visual indicator, such as a flag on someone's desk, to indicate that the lane is full. When the visual indicator is displayed, the upstream worker lends support to the downstream worker until the flow is restored.

Line Balancing

An important task in creating a future-state map for continuous flow is to determine the optimal distribution of work elements (operations) in the value stream to meet takt time. Line balancing optimizes the utilization of personnel. It balances workloads so that no one *worker* is doing too much or too little.

> ### Line Balancing
>
> Line balancing is the process by which you can evenly distribute the work elements within a value stream in order to meet takt time.

Line balancing begins with an analysis of your current state and ends with an even and fair redistribution of work throughout the process—a redistribution that focuses on ensuring that customer demand is met, but with a continuous flow mentality. The best tool to perform line balancing is the *Worker Balance Chart*.

> ### Worker Balance Chart
>
> The *Worker Balance Chart* is a visual display of the work elements, times, and workers at each location. It is used to show improvement opportunities by visually displaying the times of each work operation in relation to the total value stream cycle time and takt time.

Creating a *Worker Balance Chart* starts with a review of the cycle times and personnel assignments shown on the current-state map. For example, consider the following value stream, which has five processes (A-E), five workers, a takt time of eight minutes, and a total cycle time of 33 minutes. The first step is to create a simple flow chart of the value stream.

The next task is to create a bar chart that gives a better visual story of the current condition by showing the cycle times in each process. This current-state bar chart clearly shows a value stream that is out of balance, and where the imbalance exists (see Figure 55).

The next task is to determine the number of workers truly needed to operate this process. You do so by dividing the total process cycle time by takt time:

$$\text{\# of workers needed} = \frac{33 \text{ minutes (total process cycle time)}}{8 \text{ minutes (takt time)}} = 4.125$$

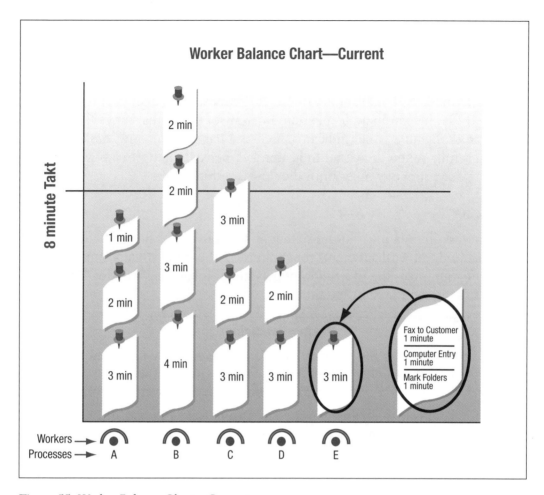

Figure 55. Worker Balance Chart—Current

A requirement of 4.125 workers makes it look like you really don't have enough work for five workers—and this is where many companies make a tremendous mistake in their interpretation of lean. Workload balancing is not about eliminating employees; it's about redistributing resources. The worker balance chart that we just created showed us two important things: the work is not distributed effectively, and there is waste in the system.

That means there is an opportunity to design an improved future state and redeploy the fifth worker. The conventions of lean thinking suggest that a decimal less than or equal to 0.5 (in this case 0.125) is a good indicator that the work elements associated with that amount of time can be eliminated. The particular worker associated with this time will be better utilized in the lean state, as you will see in the leveling phase of the process. In the improved process, each of the four remaining workers must do their share of the work within the eight-minute takt time. Thus, the total cycle time must be less than or equal to 32 minutes (four workers with an eight-minute takt time).

However, you will note that your total cycle time is 33 minutes. You must utilize standardized work (the *Standardized Work Combination Sheet* and *Standardized Work Chart* are discussed next) to ensure that the one minute of cycle time is eliminated (see Figure 56).

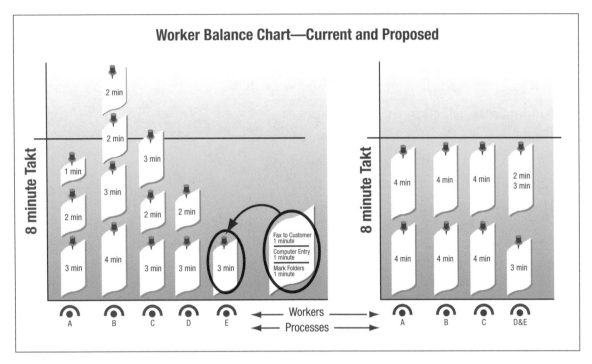

Figure 56. Worker Balance Chart—Current and Proposed

With your proposed *Worker Balance Chart* you have created a clear, visual target. However, you are probably wondering how four workers are going to complete their work when in the past five workers were having problems doing so. The tool to help you answer that question is known as *standardized work*.

Standardized Work

At this point in your planning you probably know what you want to accomplish, but you don't know *how*. Standardized work will show you how to create the continuous flow that you are looking for.

> ### *Standardized Work*
> Standardized work is an agreed-upon set of work procedures that establishes the best method and sequence for each process.

It's interesting to watch an expert perform his or her work. It's like watching an artist. But usually there's more science than art involved. For example, the greatest chefs in the world use standardized work. They use a method to keep the variables of the process constant, so that the outcome will be *predictable*. When used by a chef, standardized work produces the best, easiest, most consistent meals. When used in an administrative process it provides the best, easiest, safest, and fastest way to perform work.

Some worry that standardization stifles creativity, that it's an infringement on freedom. However, that hasn't been the experience of the companies who have implemented it. Worker creativity is always needed, first to create standards and then to hold back the onslaught of problems that challenge those standards daily. If that's not enough creative involvement, there is always continuous systematic improvement of standards.

Standardized work is a powerful tool with which to address many administrative problems. It will create an efficient workflow sequence that:

• Minimizes variations in work procedures

• Establishes the "best" practices to maintain quality

• Provides for ease of training and cross-training

• Ensures safety

• Helps workers to meet customer demand

Standardized work pinpoints activities that are required to add value in the value stream. In the analysis of the activities in the value stream, steps can be reduced, eliminated, and/or combined to ensure that the cycle time for the process is as efficient as possible. Standardized work must provide the foundation for all of your process improvement initiatives.

The tools you will use in implementing standardized work are the *Standardized Work Combination Sheet* and the *Standardized Work Chart* (see Figures 57 and 58). These are living documents that will undergo many revisions.

Standardized Work Combination Sheet

The *Standardized Work Combination Sheet* visually represents the flow of work within the process area. It specifies the exact time required for each step of the process, along with the walk or wait time between that process and the next one in the sequence.

Use the *Standardized Work Combination* sheet to understand how the cycle time for each process in the value stream compares with takt time. If the cycle time is longer than takt, the operation can be improved to meet takt.

The worksheet allows you to analyze to the level of detail required. The seconds add up to minutes, and minutes to hours. The chart in Figure 57, based on our Premiere case, clearly shows that CSRII cannot meet takt time with the current process procedures. As you can see, some small elements are included that were not collected when the current state was created.

The videocamera is probably the most useful tool to use when developing standardized work procedures. Videotape a person who is very familiar with the job and who is efficient. Review, write down, and time everything the person does, using the *Standardized Work Combination Sheet*. The team should review the results as a team and brainstorm on how to eliminate all non-value-added activities. Once the team has achieved consensus, they can revisit the video and standardized work combination sheet, incorporating the improvements. The video then becomes a job aid and training tool.

Completing the *Standardized Work Combination Sheet* is time-consuming, but your efforts will be repaid by an improved workflow.

Standardized Work Combination Sheet

Standard Work Combination

Manual	——
Walking	∿∿∿
Waiting	↕
Automatic	- - - - -

Date	6/12
Daily Reqt.	32
TaKt Time	15 Min/Order
Part Name	Orders

Operation

Customer Service Rep #2

Rev. __A__

Work Instruction No. __1__

Page __2__ of __2__

Operation Time (minutes)
(MT = Manual Time, AT = Automatic Time, WT = Walking Time)

Step #	Operation	Time		
		MT	AT	WT
1	Check Part #s 10s x 15	2.5		
2	Attach Revisions 10s x 15	2.5		
3	Assign Cust. Part # 15s x 15	3.75		
4	Estimated Price 60s x 15	15		

Totals: 23.75 + 0 + 0 = 23.75

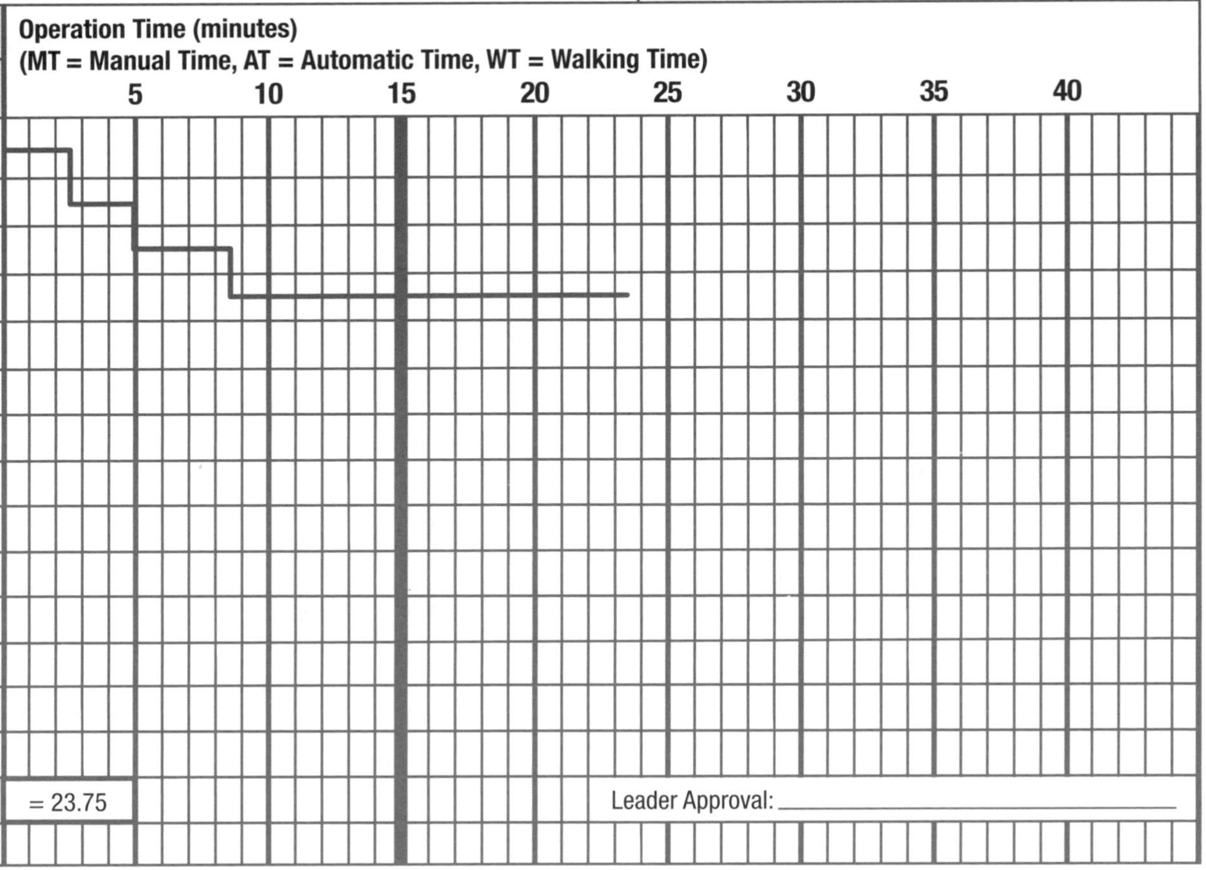

Leader Approval: _____

Figure 57. Standardized Work Combination Sheet

Standardized Work Combination Sheet

- Visually indicates the sequence and exact time for each step within a process

- Displays the process design compared to takt

- Shows the relationship between people and equipment

- Reveals waste

Standardized Work Chart

Once you have agreed on how to standardize work procedures, you create a *Standardized Work Chart*. This is a diagram that displays the sequence of work elements. It should be conspicuously displayed in the work area and updated as improvements are made.It can include all sorts of items, such as common forms, checklists, job aids, desktop organization sets, and improved filing systems.

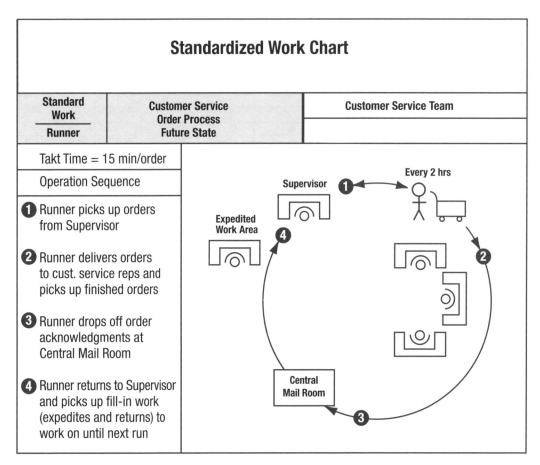

Figure 58. Standardized Work Chart

You can use a *Standardized Work Chart* to illustrate the sequence of operations within a process, including operation cycle times. Post it in the work area for all to see. This is something that is often neglected, but shouldn't be. Don't underestimate the importance of a visual office: it will enhance communication and be the foundation for further improvement initiatives.

Figure 58 shows how the *Standardized Work Chart* is used to display the flow of work in Premiere's future state. But it is also recommended that your team complete one on the current-state workflow. It's good practice, and it helps to ensure an awareness of the importance of standards.

Guidelines for Implementing Standardized Work

- Work together to determine the most efficient work methods.
- Get consensus, or adherence is unlikely.
- Do not compromise takt time—adhere to it.
- Use the *Standardized Work Combination Sheet* to understand how process cycle time compares to the takt time.
- Use the *Standardized Work Chart* to illustrate the operations in a process.

Standardized work provides a basis for consistently high levels of productivity, quality, and safety. Standards are established to reduce variation in any and all forms. As you draw your future-state map, you don't actually develop standardized work charts—this happens during the implementation process (Step 8). However, the future-state map should always show exactly where standardized work is to be implemented.

U-Shaped Cell

Changing the Layout of the Work Area

A lean work area is a self-contained, well-occupied space that includes several value-adding operations. A well-designed value stream work area optimizes the flow of work through the various processes in the minimal amount of space.

Have you ever seen a grill operator at a diner do his or her job? *That's* a good example of work-area design. Everything is in reach and in the proper order—food, plates, condiments, the toaster, and of course, the grill. All orders are prepared in sequence of delivery—first in, first out. When your burger is ready, the grill operator delivers it to you without missing a beat—and delivers it quickly.

Compare that with our office design. For example, if a work order needs to go to three people in the department during the day, and each of them sits in a different area, there will be travel time, queue time, wait time, and plenty of other time to interfere with continuous flow. Arranging the work area so that the processes or people are next to each other would eliminate much of this time—and much of the frustration.

This phase of lean implementation is often called *work area design*, but that is really a misnomer. Work area design only occurs on occasion. What's really happening at this point is a *redesign* of the physical work area in a way that will best accomplish the standardized work that the team is developing. Sometimes U-, C-, or even L-shaped work areas are the best way to accomplish this goal (see Figure 59). Whatever configuration you select will be reflected on your future-state map.

At first, work area design is a hard sell—but not for long. Once everyone sees that instead of giving up privacy they are gaining ease and efficiency, they will back this new concept completely.

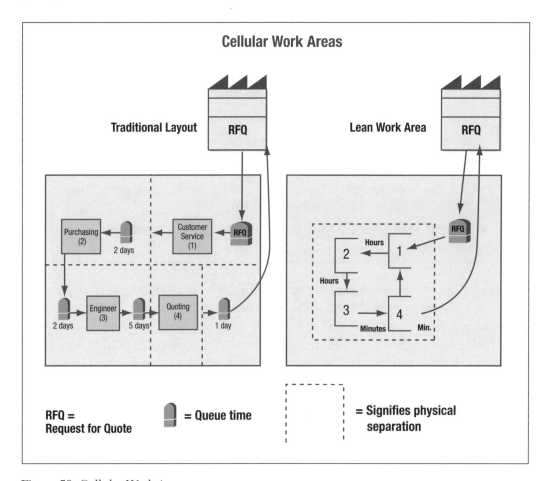

Figure 59. Cellular Work Areas

Principles of Layout Change

- Arrange processes sequentially.

- Arrange computers and equipment according to processing sequence.

- Try to use smaller machines (i.e., fax machines, printers) that fit on workers' desks.

- Perform as much cross-training as possible.

- When creating cells, place the last process as close to the first as possible.

- Set up a FIFO flow within cells.

Preparing to Map Continuous Flow

The continuous flow phase will result in dramatic change and improvement in your workplace. Still, success requires an overall plan and future-state map to guide you through these monumental changes. Before actually mapping the continuous flow phase, there are a number of things to do:

1. Review the current-state map and the demand-phase map.
2. Review the flow questions and guidelines.
3. Draw the current-state worker balance chart.
4. Draw a proposed future-state worker balance chart.
5. Review new continuous flow icons.

Just as in the previous phase, we recommend that you map the future state on a flipchart using a pencil, or on a white board using dry-erase markers. Remember that you will show on the future-state map the areas where you have introduced the improvement tools mentioned earlier. Your map is bound to change as you progress and acquire more and better information. It is good to keep a separate copy of your map at this phase, before you add leveling elements to it.

In addition to the icons you used to map the current state and the demand phase of the future state, you will need some or all of the following icons to complete the flow phase of your future-state map (see Figure 60).

Draw the Continuous-Flow-Phase Map

Mapping the continuous flow of the future state involves the following steps:

- Begin with the demand-phase map.
- Design the new workplace (work areas, locations, etc.) and draw its features in appropriate places on the map.
- Enter the number of workers and proposed cycle times of work areas on the map.
- Enter all new attributes under appropriate work areas and/or locations.
- Determine where you can apply continuous flow and show where pull should occur.
- Show where a supermarket should be placed (if required or utilized).
- Show where FIFO should occur.
- Determine where kanbans should occur and enter them on the map.
- Determine other needed improvement techniques and enter them on the map.
- Show all other communications on the map.

Remember, this map may change when you begin to level the process, so create a separate copy for reference.

Flow-Phase Icons	
Purpose	**Icon**
Kanban	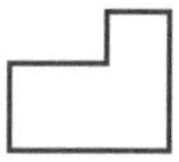
Supermarket	
U-Shaped Work Area (Cell)	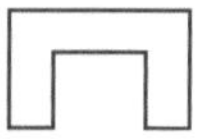
Data Base Interaction	
Physical Work-Unit Pull	
FIFO	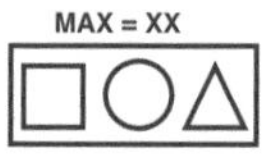 MAX = XX

Figure 60. Flow-Phase Icons

PREMIERE CASE STUDY—STEP 6–PHASE II

The team at Premiere decided that they needed to accomplish the following initiatives in the continuous flow phase:

1. Improve line balances throughout the value stream.

2. Determine where to implement standardized work procedures.

3. Utilize work area design fundamentals.

4. Decide on methods to control the workflow.

The team's first step was to complete the *Worker Balance Chart*.

Premiere's Worker Balance Chart

The team began the *Worker Balance Chart* by creating a bar chart comparing the cycle times of each operation with takt time. The line was clearly out of balance (see Figure 61).

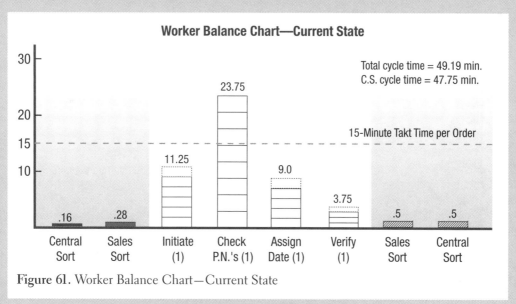

Figure 61. Worker Balance Chart—Current State

The team determined that the number of customer service workers needed to meet takt time was three, as follows.

Determining the Number of Workers

$$\text{\# of workers} = \frac{\text{Total cycle time}}{\text{Takt time}}$$

The cycle time for the customer service processes is 47.75 minutes. Takt time, as calculated in the demand-focus phase, is 15 minutes per order.

$$\text{\# of workers} = \frac{47.75 \text{ (total cycle time)}}{15 \text{ (takt time)}} = 3.18 \text{ workers}$$

Normally, if the number of workers required includes a decimal less than 0.5 (in this case .18), it is an indication that there is not enough work to keep an additional person busy. In this case, a calculation of 3.18 shows a realistic opportunity to improve the processes so that three workers can handle them.

The team decided that they needed three workers. The fourth worker would now be available for other tasks (as will be discussed in the leveling phase).

They also needed to improve the cycle time to 45 minutes or less in order to meet demand. The team set a target of 90 percent of 45 minutes, to ensure they would be able to meet demand. Their target cycle time for customer service processes is 45 minutes × 90 percent or 40.9 minutes.

The team completed the worker balance chart by creating a bar chart of the future state (see Figure 62).

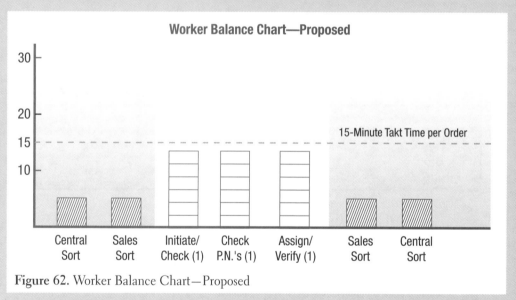

Figure 62. Worker Balance Chart—Proposed

Standardized Work

The team decided that the *Standardized Work Combination Sheet* and *Standardized Work Chart* would be utilized to improve cycle time, standardize the three remaining jobs, and allow for maximum job flexibility. The team thought that they could develop common forms, formats, and set patterns of work for tasks to be performed on a repeatable basis.

Work Area Design

Now that they had determined that only three workers were needed, the team had to decide how to design the physical workplace. Desks for customer service representatives would be grouped in a U-shaped cell so that hand-offs were immediate. This would reduce the four-hour queue time that normally occurred between each process. Office rearrangement into a U-shaped work area also allowed for increased communications, sharing of resources, and reduced travel.

Other Methods to Control Workflow

The team decided on the following:

1. All forms, desktop folders, and customer specifications were to be located on each CSR's desk at exact locations. This would allow handoffs and pick-ups to occur quickly and easily. This will become a FIFO system.

2. The orders would be distributed from the mail cart to the customer service supervisor. They would then be allocated to the appropriate work area.

3. A supermarket would be used to hold the various types of office supplies in a kanban system.

4. The customer service team would hold morning "shift start" meetings to assist one another if workloads required it. A shift start is normally a five- to seven-minute meeting at the beginning of the day to ensure that everyone is on the same page and to determine if changes need to be made early in the day—rather than at 4:00 p.m.

5. They would rearrange the work areas so that all three CSRs would be sitting within the same barrier-free area (U-shaped).

6. They would create the *Standardized Work Combination Sheet* and *Standardized Work Chart* to further define and improve cycle time.

7. They would post the *Standardized Work Chart* on the visual board.

8. They would utilize the *Standardized Work Combination Sheet* as the basis for continuous improvement.

9. They would e-mail order acknowledgments to customers directly from order processing. This would ensure that customers would receive an acknowledgment in a timely manner. While they would still need to send paper acknowledgments by mail, there would be a future opportunity to eliminate this activity if customers would agree to forego a hardcopy.

The team completed the continuous flow phase by drawing the map and filling in all of the appropriate attributes for the work area that they created (see Figure 63).

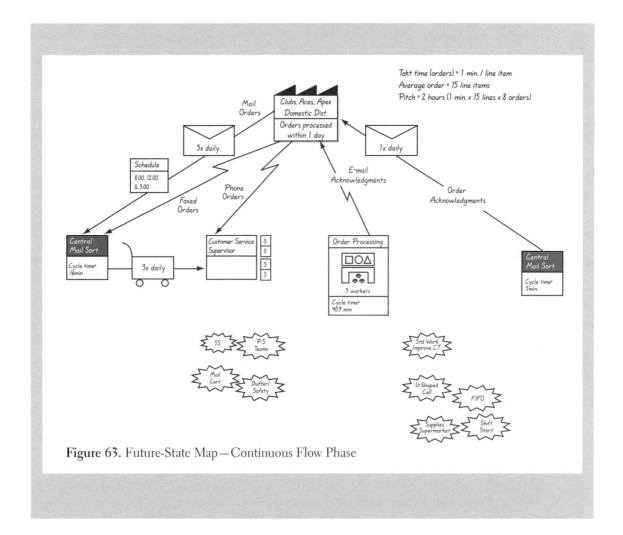

Figure 63. Future-State Map—Continuous Flow Phase

Keys to Successful Implementation

In order to implement the continuous flow phase successfully, the core implementation team must accomplish the following:

1. Understand continuous flow.

You must study the requirements and opportunities of a continuous flow workplace because it is a different environment from those most people are accustomed to working in. Learn what the new tools have to offer.

2. Remember work area design.

Remember, what really occurs at this point is a redesign of the physical work area in a way that will best accomplish the standardized work that the team is developing. U-, C-, or L-shaped *work areas* may be the best way to accomplish this goal.

3. Always control upstream work.

Upstream work, or work that occurs before it is required by a downstream process in the value stream, will determine the time at, and condition in which, work arrives at a particular place.

4. Plan for training and communication.

People don't just learn new things accidentally. You need a plan to teach them. A plan is as simple as knowing the following about training and communicating:

- What
- To whom
- When
- How

5. Remember people and how they react to change.

Keep in mind that the lean implementation is a period of transition. You are changing people's jobs, and their workspace. Always consider people in every decision. Do a lot of listening.

Step 6–Phase III. Map the Future State— Leveling

In the previous chapter, "Map the Future State—Continuous Flow Phase," you examined how you could design continuous flow into your future state. In this section, you will continue to design your future state by adding to your map the elements that will help you level your work.

> ### *Leveling*
>
> Leveling involves evenly distributing the work required to fulfill customer demand over a period of time (i.e., week, day, or hour).

If work is not leveled, work areas will experience times when they fall behind in processing (causing other work areas to wait), and other times when they are waiting for work. Your efforts in this phase will apply specific measures and techniques to ensure the balanced or smooth meeting of customer requirements throughout the day. You will:

1. Review customer demand through takt time and pitch.

2. Review or create the pull (kanban) system.

3. Create a load leveling box, if required.

4. Create a delivery and pick-up system.

> ### *Questions for Focus on Leveling*
>
> Application of the leveling phase can be summarized by the following questions:
>
> - How will work units be grouped to move through the value stream in a way that:
>   - Best represents customer demand?
>   - Provides for process flexibility?
> - How will kanban cards be distributed to ensure that integrity is maintained throughout the value stream?
> - Where in the process will you schedule work requirements?
> - What other improvement methods will help you achieve leveling?

Leveling in Restaurants

Restaurants providing quality service understand the concept of leveling and use it to seat customers to balance the amount of work given to waiters. The goal is to seat each customer as rapidly as possible and then provide the quickest, most attentive service. If restaurants don't use leveling, there will often be customers waiting for service, feeling that they have a very poor waiter. But the waiter is probably working frantically, never catching up. The dining experience for the customer isn't pleasant; the waiter is probably getting angry at the host(ess); and the host(ess) is mad at the manager for hiring such poor waiters. *Whose fault is it?*

In another part of the restaurant there are probably vacant tables, with waiters feeling they are having a slow night and not making enough in tips. And you can probably bet that there are frustrated customers waiting to be seated. Meanwhile, they can see those empty seats and are probably arguing with the host(ess).

Much of this can be avoided. Let's see how. Note, though, that this is a simplified explanation, and that many restaurants operate beyond this simple example.

The first task is to evenly distribute the work, just as we did in the office with work area design. The dining room is divided into sections, not unlike work areas in the office. Some work areas may seat more people than others, based on numbers of tables or other issues. These work assignments seem simple on the surface, but they are critical to the leveling process. By assigning these tables, the manager is saying that the waiter can handle this number of tables at any one time. The specific tables given are significant in that each table might have a different number of chairs, be located in a different place, and have other important characteristics. In other words, based on history, the manager knows how much work each work area will require. The work area is *not* based on individual skills of waiters, or preferred areas (say, the better tables by the windows), which may not seat as many people. It is based on standards, on what *should* occur in a work area. A matrix that reflects this grid is studied until all tables are covered and each person has been assigned an even amount of potential customers (see Figure 64).

Work Area	Table Assignments
A	1, 2, 3
B	4, 5, 6, 7
C	8, 9, 10, 11

Figure 64. Table Assignments Example

At this point it's important to mention that all of the principles of the customer demand and continuous flow phases apply here, especially standardized work. So let's assume that these phases have been done and we're ready to enter into the leveling phase. The next task is to spread the work out over time. A good restaurant knows its history—when people arrive for dinner and how long they stay. It knows that most customers stay for about 75 minutes. That means that they can plan for three seatings: 5:30 p.m., 7:00 p.m., and 8:30 p.m., giving workers five minutes to change the table for a new seating. Of course, people can come whenever they want, but this is how they will plan, including reservations. A leveling matrix like the one below is created.

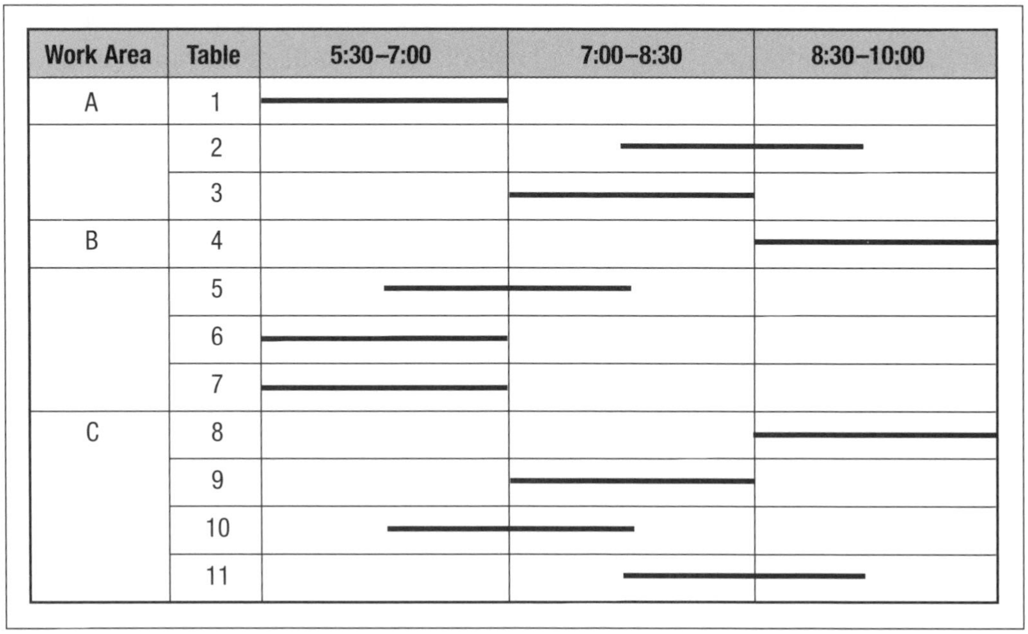

Work Area	Table	5:30–7:00	7:00–8:30	8:30–10:00
A	1	————		
	2		————	————
	3		————	
B	4			————
	5	——	————	
	6	————		
	7	————		
C	8			————
	9		————	
	10	——	————	
	11		——	————

Figure 65. Restaurant Leveling Matrix Example

Now they can evenly distribute customers throughout the dining room over the entire night. As people are seated, the slot is filled. When people call for reservations, names can be easily plugged in. The manager can, at a glance, see if seating is balanced.

Restaurant seating demonstrates that the level distribution of work requires a managed and controlled method, one that breaks work up into small pieces and distributes it over time.

But don't forget, all we've done so far is get our customers seated. Leveling work goes far beyond merely planning work: we also must *make the plan work* on the restaurant floor. For example, how long should changing tables between seatings take? A changeover team should be ready to immediately remove all used dishes, silverware, and linens, and reset the table. The team should have a cart with them with everything they need on it. It should take them less than five minutes.

Administrative lean gives us effective tools to implement leveling in the office. Let's turn to them now.

Leveling Administrative Work

Leveling administrative work means distributing the load over time to evenly distribute that work. If you do not level work, some work areas will be too busy and fall behind (causing idle time downstream).

When we focused on demand, we talked about the importance of takt time, which is a way to monitor whether you are meeting customer demand. To meet customer demand you must establish a method for matching the pace of work to the pace of demand (or takt time) and still be able to efficiently plan for the needed resources. That method is leveling.

The Need for Leveling

Let's assume that an accounts payable department has already implemented the demand phase of value stream management, as well as standardized work and work area design. They even have an in-process supermarket, where three workers who process invoices pick up their waiting work (assigned by alphabetical order).

So what's the problem? Why do they need leveling? The problem is that there is no balance in the work. Invoices don't come in for payment based on the alphabet. Some days, Worker A has too much work, and Worker B doesn't have enough. But it's not always easy to see the imbalance. A method is needed to level the work.

Why not use a true, one-piece-flow system? Why not throw out the alphabet system and have workers pull one invoice at a time, and only one? One problem was that the three workers could never get together for meetings; somebody was always busy. And they always felt pressure. There was always an order that needed to be pulled and processed. After all, they did have other responsibilities besides processing invoices. The drumbeat of takt time was a little too demanding. A system was needed that would absorb and fulfill customer demand, and still allow enough flexibility for them to do their other work.

A true one-piece-flow system would create other imbalances in the value stream. The manager who has to approve the payments would not be able to plan this portion of his work very well. There would be an ebb and flow of work, based on the speed of each individual piece of work by the workers. This would create an imbalance for the department clerk, whose job it is to prepare the payments for the mail.

The invoices, or "work units," must maintain a certain pace so the downstream procedures will be able to process them. Most likely, it would not be one invoice at time. The value stream process owners must look at the overall flow and determine the time and the amount of work units to flow.

Begin with Customer Demand

Let's address customer demand first. The department has to accept that paying bills on time is important to the company. For them, the vendor becomes the customer. When the department implemented the demand phase of VSM, they calculated their takt time as being the processing of one invoice every 4.2 minutes (based on 420 available minutes for a requirement of 100 invoices per day).

Pitch

As we've already seen, using takt time alone to monitor customer demand won't work. We need something that serves the office better. Pitch will do the trick. Pitch modifies takt to account for other office resource issues, but still provides a rhythm to work that has its roots in customer demand. Pitch is determined by multiplying takt time by the number of work units required at any one time.

To determine pitch, the accounts payable department has to decide the best small work lots to work in. For them, since there are no customer shipping requirements, these small lots are best determined by time. The best way to plan their day is to determine the number of invoices normally needed in an hour, and identify that as a lot. Since takt time is one invoice each 4.2 minutes, pitch is 14.3 invoices per hour.

Visible Pitch Board

Now the department can create a visible pitch board.

> ### Visible Pitch Board
>
> A visual control method that will control the flow of work throughout the day.

The visible pitch board separates the work into pitch—14 invoices per hour. Then it goes further. It shows how each person in the value stream receives his or her portion of the work. Note that the actual pitch is 14.3 orders per hour. To compensate for the 0.3, the team handles an extra invoice at 9 a.m. and 1 p.m. (see Figure 66).

Visible Pitch Board—Accounts Payable Department								
Time →	9 a.m.	10 a.m.	11 a.m.	Noon	1 p.m.	2 p.m.	3 p.m.	4 p.m.
Worker A	5	4	4		5	4	4	4
Worker B	5	5	5		5	5	5	5
Worker C	5	5	5		5	5	5	5
Pitch	15	14	14		15	14	14	14

Figure 66. Visible Pitch Board–Accounts Payable Department

Notice that Worker A routinely receives four invoices per hour, and Workers B and C receive five. That's because Worker A has the added responsibility of answering questions and phone calls. He's been there the longest and seems able to answer any inquiry. He's been nicknamed "Know-it Freddie." The team has one hour to complete all 14 invoices before another 14 will be delivered.

Creation of a visible pitch board doesn't ensure that you will operate with a "pull" mentality. For that you need a kanban system. Don't forget, in leveling we do not want to push too much work into the system. If demand is beginning to exceed capacity, we need to know it immediately so that we can respond.

Review Standardized Work

When they implemented continuous flow, the accounts payable department standardized the work of invoice processing. They created kanban folders that would act as vehicles for all work (invoices) from the time it entered the department to the time it was approved by the manager, then mailed by the clerk. On the inside left cover of every folder was a standardized work chart along with a process flow chart, clearly stating the procedures and any other needed information.

Color-Coded Kanban Folders

Since work was to be distributed separately among three workers, folders were color- coded:

- Worker A: red
- Worker B: blue
- Worker C: green

Every hour, each worker received a folder with his or her work in it, and any other messages or needed information. That folder is clearly marked with the pitch time within which it is to be processed.

Mailbox System

There is an important rule that makes this system work: *Don't push too much work into the system.* Kanban accompanied by a mailbox system accomplishes this.

At each desk is a mailbox for receiving the folder, based on the visible pitch board. There is also a box for sending it to the next operation. For example, at 11 a.m., Worker B will receive a folder with five invoices to process. That assumes that Worker B has "pulled" the folder from the box that was delivered at 10 a.m. If she hasn't, the delivery cannot be made, and back-up procedures must automatically be followed. In the case of the accounts payable department, those procedures are:

- Find out why the folder wasn't pulled and whether the assigned worker can take it within 10 minutes.
- Get help from the team.
- "Bump" the work to the supervisor to process.

Another issue involves the "out" box. At 11 a.m., if the folder that belongs in the out box is not there, work will begin to slow downstream. So automatic procedures need to be in place for that as well.

As you can see, kanban provides visual control based on customer demand and teamwork. But leveling doesn't stop there.

Heijunka Boxes

The heijunka, or leveling, box is a physical device used to level work volume *and variety* over a specified period.

Remember, the pitch board was utilized to distribute the work load by volume only. Here, the load is leveled with consideration for the most efficient use of people and resources. In a lean system, the heijunka box is often the best place to input information on daily work requirements.

In a sense, the heijunka box is the post office for the value stream, and the runner (discussed next) is the mailman. Kanban cards or folders are placed in slots corresponding to the pitch increments in which work units are to be released to the next downstream process and subsequently replenished (see Figure 67).

Heijunka Box – Accounts Payable

Figure 67. Heijunka Box

The above example shows how variety (e.g., check requests, credit memos, and expense reports) could be added to utilize the heijunka system to its fullest. Again, you would normally start with a visible pitch board (which is the same as heijunka, but without any variety). Do not get hung up in the nomenclature; work to improve the flow.

The Runner

The runner is used to pace the work or movement of information, ensuring that pitch is maintained.

Runner

The Runner
A worker who ensures that pitch is maintained. The runner covers a designated route within the pitch period, picks up kanban cards or folders and work units, and delivers them to their appropriate destinations.

At the specified time, the runner removes the kanban card or folder, and the work unit is delivered to the next process. If a work unit is not ready for pickup, the problem is immediately identified. The runner can then assist the process by communicating to the manager or supervisor, summoning additional support, or otherwise making the problem known and providing for an immediate resolution.

Runner Qualifications
• Understands value stream process requirements
• Communicates well
• Understands lean concepts
• Understands the importance of takt and pitch
• Works efficiently and precisely
• Is innovative and resourceful

Runners play an important role in proactive problem solving. Because they continuously monitor the functioning of a line or work area as well as pitch (or takt time), runners are closely attuned to how well the value stream is fulfilling customer requirements. They are in a unique position to help prevent small problems before they become big problems that seriously disrupt process flow.

Remember that leveling occurs *after* you have achieved continuous flow. It is a refinement of your lean design. You may find that specific techniques implemented earlier will be eliminated as you successfully level production.

Mapping the Future State—Leveling Phase

Now that you are familiar with the techniques of leveling, it is time to draw the portion of the future-state map that applies to leveling. Answering the following questions will guide you through the process. Then you will make appropriate adjustments to complete the map. Begin with the map you completed after focusing on flow, and build from there.

1. What are the minimum work-unit group sizes the system maintains?
2. What types of kanban cards or folders will you use?
3. How will kanban cards or folders be distributed?
4. Will you use a heijunka box?
5. What will be the runner's route?

In addition to the icons you used in Steps 4 and 6 to map the current state and the customer demand and continuous flow phases of the future state, you will need the following icons to complete the leveling phase of your future-state map.

Leveling-Phase Icons	
Purpose	**Icon**
Heijunka Box Volume / Variety	XOXO
Runner Route	
Pitch Board	

Figure 68. Leveling-Phase Icons

PREMIERE CASE STUDY—STEP 6–PHASE III

The team at Premiere decided that they needed to accomplish the following initiatives in the leveling phase:

1. Develop and implement a kanban system.
2. Create a load-leveling (heijunka) box.
3. Implement a runner system.

Kanban

The team decided that for the future state to be effective, they would create a kanban system of folders, with local delivery and receiving boxes at each desk. The folders would be color-coded by customer.

Load-Leveling (Heijunka) Box

The customer service supervisor needed to level each work delivery, and needed a heijunka box in which to distribute the orders (see Figure 69).

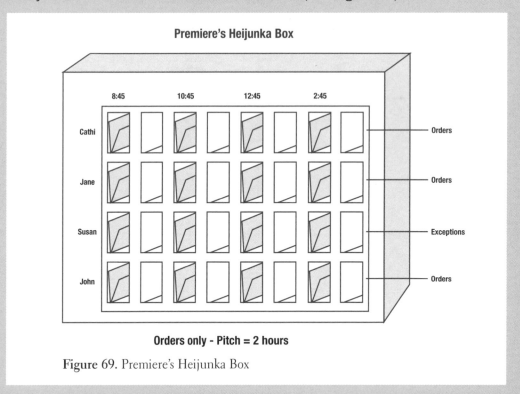

Figure 69. Premiere's Heijunka Box

The box would be loaded in two-hour increments based on the capacity of order processing (one minute/line item/person), expedited orders (10 minutes/order), and returned work units (four minutes/order). The kanban folder would be used to load the heijunka box and feed the work areas. The team determined that the cycle time for loading the heijunka box was one minute per order.

They added this information to the future-state map (see Figure 70).

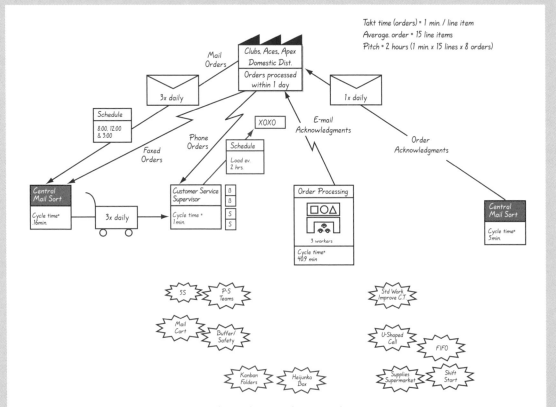

Figure 70. Future-State Map—Leveling Phase with Heijunka Box

Runner

Since there were currently four workers in the value stream, but only three will be needed to process new orders in the future, the fourth worker would be designated as the runner. This person would also handle the exceptions (expedited orders and returns), and would be available as an additional resource for handling overflow work in order processing. The team also decided that the runner's job would be rotated on a monthly basis.

The runner's route would be as follows:

1. Pick up orders from the heijunka box every two hours, after it is loaded by the customer service supervisor.

2. Deliver the orders to the customer service reps and pick up finished orders.

3. Drop off order acknowledgments at the central mailroom.

4. Return to the heijunka box and pick up exceptions and overflow orders to work on until the next run.

The runner would also play a key role in signaling whether customer service was falling behind in order processing. As he or she made the run every two hours, it would be easy to see if anyone was falling behind. New work would not be delivered to that customer service representative. Instead, the kanban folder of new work would be returned to its time slot in the heijunka box, signaling the customer service supervisor that action may need to be taken to deal with the overflow.

The team completed the leveling phase by drawing the new information on the future-state map. They also added the new step chart and calculated the new total cycle time, lead time, and value-added percentage (see Figure 71).

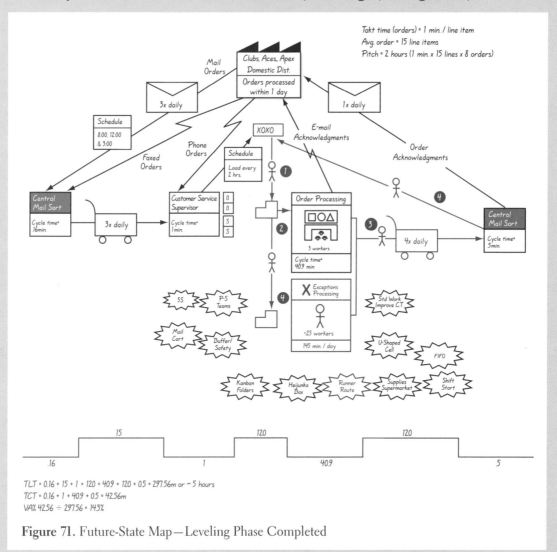

Figure 71. Future-State Map—Leveling Phase Completed

They entered onto the storyboard the lean tools they would be using to create the future state (see Figure72).

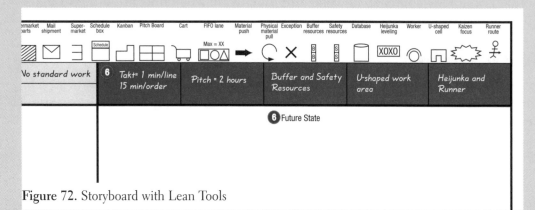

Figure 72. Storyboard with Lean Tools

Keys to Successful Implementation

1. Understand leveling and the tools of leveling.

Leveling is a unique approach to work. You initially may be reluctant, but give it a chance—it has proven to be successful time and time again.

2. Stay in sequence.

Be sure that the tools in the demand and flow phases have been used in the correct sequence and in the appropriate places before applying leveling. In some cases you won't have to use leveling. In others, how you will use leveling will change as needed.

3. Stay simple and low-tech.

Do you remember the old saying, "garbage in, garbage out," regarding computers? It means that your computer system is only as good as the information you enter into it. This applies to your leveling system as well. We have found that simple, low-tech systems have the longest life and offer the greatest rewards.

4. Be flexible and responsive to any issues that arise.

People are the key: if they understand what is going on, and feel that management is supportive, the entire planning and implementation will proceed well.

Step 7. Create Kaizen Plans

Kaizen derives from "kai," meaning to take apart, and "zen," meaning to make good. Thus, by using kaizen, you take apart your processes in order to make them better. Kaizen plans can be related to an entire project, or to something as simple as the first phase of 5S. It is the process that needs to be in place to ensure that the improvements are sustained and the office worker's efforts acknowledged. In Step 6 you designed your new state. Step 7 is a call to action.

Create a kaizen plan in a way that makes it user-friendly. The first thing to remember is that you should not worry about creating a *perfect* future-state map or a *perfect* kaizen plan. The plan need only be good enough to get you started. You will modify it as you implement improvements and gain a practical understanding of lean methods. This chapter gives you guidelines for creating a workable kaizen plan.

Strategic Links

Begin Step 7 by reviewing the business reason for conducting value stream management activities. Ask questions like the following to confirm that there is a strategic intent behind implementing lean methods:

1. Why are you implementing lean in this value stream?

2. What impact will implementing lean methods have on your customers?

3. What quality improvements will you achieve?

4. What cost savings will you achieve?

5. What strategic objectives does this project relate to?

Reviewing the lean metrics you identified in Step 5 will help you formulate your responses. Answering these questions thoroughly will help you gain approval for your plan during the catchball process.

This is also the time to set proposed target metrics and add them to the storyboard. Review the information from your future-state plan and the strategic links you identified, and determine six-month target metrics. These will also help drive your kaizen planning.

Plan Your Implementation Phases

It should be obvious that you can't implement your value stream improvement ideas all at once. You need to break them into phases. We recommend that you use the same three phases you used to plan the future state:

1. Plan how you will ensure that you are able to meet customer demand.

2. Plan how you will improve the process flow.

3. Plan how you will level the work.

Using this planning sequence allows for the most effective and least costly implementation of kaizen plans. For example, once you truly understand customer demand you may gain additional insight into arranging operations into more efficient work areas, and you should modify your plans accordingly. Similarly, the whole nature of a leveling system may change once you have some real experience with continuous flow and, again, you will need to modify your plans based on your new understanding.

The Monthly Kaizen Plan

You can begin the process by creating a detailed monthly kaizen plan showing implementation of the main elements in the different implementation phases (demand, flow, and leveling). Create an item in the monthly plan for each kaizen focus on your map. A blank example of a monthly plan is shown in Figure 73.

Milestones

Now that you have the basic structure of your plan segmented into demand, flow, and leveling phases, determine specific implementation items, or "milestones," for each segment, its implementation sequence, and other details.

Milestones

A milestone is an activity that has, or should have, a scheduled completion date or time, and that has a major effect on the timing or completion of a project.

A milestone should also be measurable in terms of the extent of its completion.

Monthly Kaizen Plan Worksheet

Value Stream: _____   Date: _____

Phase	Specific Event	Six-Month Schedule					
		J	F	M	A	M	J
D							
E							
M							
A							
N							
D							
F							
L							
O							
W							
L							
E							
V							
E							
L							

△ = Start Date   ➤ = Expected Duration   ▲ = Planned Completion

Figure 73. Monthly Kaizen Plan Worksheet

Kaizen Milestone Charts

Kaizen Milestone Charts are similar to your monthly plan in that they show implementation and completion of activities over time. *Kaizen Milestone Charts* are, however, much more detailed. An example of a milestone chart is shown in the Premiere case study that follows. Note the symbols used to mark progress toward achieving the milestones: an open triangle signifies the start date, a line with an arrow marks the expected duration of implementation, and a solid triangle marks the completion of a milestone.

Catchball

After you complete your storyboard, it is time to play catchball again and get buy-in for your plans. Here is where all your hard effort—particularly the effort to generate kaizen plans—will really pay off. The storyboard summarizes your plans for a lean transformation of the target value stream. You will most likely be presenting your plan to high-level managers. If you show that you have planned the future state carefully and also given careful thought to *how* the plan is to be implemented systematically, the catchball process will go smoothly.

A good way for the core implementation team members to prepare for the meeting at which they present the storyboard to upper management is by assuring they can answer the following questions (which are the same as those presented at the beginning of this chapter):

- Why are we implementing lean in this value stream?
- What impact will implementing lean methods have on our customers?
- What quality improvements will we achieve?
- What cost savings will we achieve?
- How does this project relate to our strategic objectives?

Being able to answer such questions shows upper management that you have a firm understanding of the strategic intent behind the lean transformation.

PREMIERE CASE STUDY—STEP 7

In order to review strategic links, the team looked at their team charter as well as their storyboard with completed future-state map. They established six-month targets for each of the baseline metrics determined in Step 5 (see Figure 74).

Lean Measurable	Baseline Measure	Target (six months)
Total order cycle time	49.19 minutes	42.6 minutes
Total order lead time	4.5 days	1 day
On-time delivery (% orders entered during 8-hour period)	32%	99%
Number of defective parts per million	4691 DPPM	1,000 DPPM
Lean assessment	14	24

Figure 74. Lean Measurables, Baseline and Target Measures

Next they reviewed the kaizen focus icons they had mapped during the demand, flow, and leveling stages of the future state. They created a monthly kaizen plan showing the timeframes for each kaizen event, and then proceeded to create a more detailed kaizen milestone chart specifying the team member responsible for coordinating each task, as well as the start and completion weeks for each (see Figure 75).

Kaizen Milestone Chart

Value Stream:	Value Stream Team Members:	Date:	Page 1 of 1
Family I	Ron, Lori, Debbie, Jane, Susan, M.B., M.D.		

ITEM	TASK	ASSIGN TO	SEPT.	OCT.	NOV.	DEC.	JAN.	FEB.	MAR.
	Demand								
1	5S	M.B.	▲→						
2	P.S. Team—Buffer/Safety Resource Plan	D.W.	▲→						
3	P.S. Team—Mail Cart	S.L.	▲→						
	Flow								
4	Desk FIFO Lanes	L.D.		▲→					
5	Supermarket (Office supplies)	D.W.		▲→					
6	Shift Starts	R.W.		▲→					
7	U-Shaped Work Area	J.H.			▲→				
8	Standardized Work	M.B.			▲→				
9	Kanban Flow (Folders)	L.D.			▲→				
	Leveling								
10	Heijunka	D.W.					▲→		
11	Runner Route	D.W.						▲→	

▲ = Start Date   Estimated Time to Completion →   ▲ = Completed   Past Due !   - - - - - - - - = Four-Week Month

Figure 75. Kaizen Milestone Chart

They updated the storyboard with their target metrics and their main kaizen proposals and timeframes. They were now ready for a round of catchball with management before proceeding with implementation.

			⑤ Metrics										**⑦**
Lead Time		Total CycleTime		On-time Delivery		DPPM		Assessment					
Base	Proposed	Base	Proposed	Base	Proposed	Base	Proposed	Base	Proposed	Base	Proposed	Dem	
4.5 days	1 day	49.19 min	42.6 min	32%	99%	4,691	1,000	14	24			Flow	
												Flow	
												Flow	
												Flow	
												Leve	

1. Commit to Lean
2. Choose the Value Stream
3. Learn about Lean
4. Map the Current State

	⑦ Kaizen Proposal	**⑧**			
		1st	2nd	3rd	4th
posed	Demand – 5S, Buffer and Safety Resources, and Mail Cart				
	Flow – FIFO, Supermarket, and Shift Starts				
	Flow – U-shaped Work Area				
	Flow – Standardized Work				
	Flow – Kanban Folders				
	Leveling – Heijunka and Runner Route				

5. Identify Lean Metrics   ◯ Started
6. Map the Future State   ⬤ Complete
7. Create Kaizen Plans   ⊗ Past Due
8. Implement Kaizen Plans

Figure 76. Storyboard with Proposed Metrics and Kaizen Proposal

Keys to Successful Implementation

Remember that planning is primarily about managing action. Here are some guidelines for effective kaizen planning:

- **Be realistic**—especially regarding completion dates.
- **Play catchball**—get buy-in from all stakeholders.
- **Be detailed**—detailed enough to promote clear communication and understanding.
- **Communicate**—show proposals to everyone connected to the value stream.
- **Make it visual**—use the storyboard.
- **Recognize good work**—make sure people's contributions are recognized.
- **Be sure to celebrate**—you've done a tremendous amount of work; you deserve to celebrate (celebration is in fact an important way to recognize contributions).

Step 8. Implement Kaizen Plans

The final step in your lean transformation is to *do it!* In Step 6 you created a new design, and in Step 7 you developed an organized, systematic kaizen plan to make that design a reality. Now it's time to make it happen.

In our experience, there are three phases to implementation of kaizen plans: preparation, implementation, and follow-up.

The preparation phase took place in Step 7. All the planning and preparation that you have done so far should allow you to proceed to the implementation phase with enthusiasm and confidence. However, remember that when implementation begins in earnest, kaizen activities will have an impact on virtually everyone connected to the target value stream.

Recommendations for Coping with Change

Change—even change for the better—is difficult for most people. But the more that people understand what's going on, the easier it is for them to deal with their anxieties, whether the change is significant or minor. Here are some recommendations for managing and coping with the anxieties that are bound to present themselves as you proceed:

1. **Communicate, communicate, communicate!** Make sure that everyone upstream and downstream of the area where a kaizen event is taking place knows what is happening and why. A brief explanation by a leader or supervisor may be all that is necessary for people to feel that information is not being withheld from them.

2. **Address negative behavior early in the implementation.** If someone does not seem to be going along or displays negative behavior, talk to that person privately. Listen to his or her concerns and work to resolve them. Focused, active listening is an acquired skill. People's feelings are very real to them, and you must take care not to diminish those feelings by interrupting people while they are speaking. Hear them out; show that you genuinely care. *Then* respond. Explain how the improvement effort will make the company stronger, which will potentially make everyone's future brighter and more prosperous. If possible, assure people that no one will lose his or her job as a result of improving the value stream.

3. **Do not let a problem stop the process.** Perhaps an unforeseen problem makes it impossible to complete a kaizen event. Acknowledge the problem and reschedule the event for completion as soon as the problem is resolved. Do not look at the delay as a failure, but as a detour in a fascinating journey!

4. **Consider each kaizen event an experiment.** Let's say that a team is redesigning a work area, but you underestimated how much time it would take and didn't anticipate

the impact it would have on a neighboring department. You *will* make some mistakes. Learn from them and move on! For example, one way to repair this would be to identify the parts of the design that could be done without impacting the other department, and then proceed from there.

5. Reward and recognize people's efforts. Practice mutual trust and respect, and treat people with honesty and integrity every day.

6. Be present. The value stream champion and top managers should go to the work area regularly to encourage people and to find out what they can do to support improvement efforts.

7. Be flexible. Things the team members didn't plan for will appear, and things they did plan for won't turn out the way they expected. But all are opportunities for learning more about the department's processes and the people who are doing the work.

Keep the Big Picture in Mind

As you progress, keep the big picture in mind. Refer to the storyboard frequently to explain to people how using the structured value stream management process makes extraordinary achievements possible. Big changes to the value stream, combined with small incremental improvements, create a fast, flexible, customer-driven process with little waste.

What does it mean to have a fast, flexible process? If you are currently assigning work by the week, assign it by the day. If you assign work by the day, consider assigning work by the hour.

Kaizen Events

The focus of a kaizen event can be as simple as creating visual controls for a mailroom or as difficult as rearranging a large, complex value stream into many open-area departments with multiple workers. The more difficult the kaizen event, the more time will be required to plan it.

> ### *Kaizen Event*
>
> A team event dedicated to quick implementation of a lean method in a particular area over a short time period.

A dedicated kaizen event is defined as a total resource commitment to the work area. For more involved and resource-consuming events, always plan well, know exactly how long the implementation will last, and review progress with the team immediately after the event.

As implementation occurs you will get some real feedback from employees because they are now actually living with the changes. So, remember, as you change the work unit and information flow and the way people work, keep in mind that your real purpose is to support the people who create value for your customers. One of your objectives is to receive ideas and suggestions for value stream improvements from employees. They are the ones who create value for your customers and best know the details of the value stream.

Finally, be patient and realistic. At the company that provided the data for the Premiere case study, the value stream transformation took nearly a year to complete. The hoped for time frame was six months, but it took longer due to:

- An unexpected increase in customer orders—a record sales year—with no increase in staff.

- The need to spend additional time in understanding how the volume and variety of orders could be broken down into a pitch increment.

- The recognition that the entire customer service organization needed to be redesigned.

Becoming lean *does* make a difference.

Kaizen Events: Keys to Success

- Identify the objectives of the event and be sure to communicate them clearly to the kaizen team before team members go out onto the floor.

- Identify exactly who will attend, when they will attend, and what their roles will be.

- Define the scope of the team's efforts.

- Identify any training that needs to take place during the event.

- Use the *Kaizen Milestone Chart* to determine the projected completion date for the event.

- Determine special needs that must be resolved to prevent problems from occurring.

- Draft an agenda for the duration of the event; include specific start and stop times.

- Create a team charter for any new teams.

Wrap-up

For success to occur in your organization, people must continually look for ways to improve the entire value stream. Cultivate a kaizen environment every day by recognizing and rewarding people's efforts and treating them with dignity and respect.

Also, remember that not everything always goes according to plan. Expect the unexpected, and adjust your plans accordingly.

Good luck on the road to becoming a lean office!

Glossary

5S System: An improvement process, originally summarized by five Japanese words beginning with S, to create a workplace that will meet the criteria of visual control and lean production.

Benchmarking: A structured approach to identifying a world-class process, then gathering relevant information and applying it within your own organization to improve a similar process.

Buffer resources: A means of meeting customer demand when customer ordering patterns, or takt times, vary.

Catchball: A give-and-take activity performed between different levels of the organization to make sure that critical information on goals and objectives as well as feedback is passed back and forth.

Continuous flow: The ideal state characterized by the ability to replenish a single work unit that has been "pulled" downstream. In practice, continuous flow is synonymous with just-in-time (JIT), which ensures that both internal and external customers receive *only* what is needed, *just when* it is needed, and in the *exact amounts* needed.

Core implementation team: A group of people chartered with planning the details of a lean plan through implementation of the eight-step value stream management process.

Cycle time: The time that elapses from the beginning of a process or operation until its completion.

Demand/customer demand: The quantity of work units required by a customer. See also *takt time*.

Extended team members: Individuals who provide special skills or expertise to the core implementation team but who are not responsible for implementation.

FIFO: First in, first out (FIFO) is a work-control method used to ensure that the oldest work (first in) is the first to be processed (first out).

Flow: The movement of material or information. Businesses are successful to the extent that they are able to move material and information with as few disruptions as possible — preferably none.

Heijunka or load leveling: Balancing the amount of work to be done (the load) during a day with the capacity to complete the work. A heijunka system distributes work in proportions based on demand, factoring in volume and variety.

Heijunka box: A physical device used to level production volume and variety over a specified time period (usually one day). The box is divided into slots that represent pitch increments. The slots are loaded with kanbans that represent customer orders. The order in which kanbans are loaded into the box is determined based on volume and variety.

Just-in-time (JIT): A paradigm which ensures that customers receive *only* what is needed, *just when* it is needed, and in the *exact amounts* needed. See also *continuous flow.*

Kaizen: Small daily improvements performed by everyone. *Kai* means "take apart" and *zen* means "make good." The point of kaizen implementation is the total elimination of waste.

Kaizen event: A team event dedicated to quick implementation of a lean method in a particular area over a short time period.

Kaizen plans: Lean improvement proposals presented to management by the team, following their analysis of their current state map and mapping their future state.

Kanban: A control card at the heart of a pull system. The card is a means of communicating upstream precisely what is required (in terms of work specifications and quantity) at the time it is required.

Lean: A paradigm based on the fundamental goal of eliminating waste and maximizing flow.

Lean enterprise: An organization that fully understands, communicates, implements, and sustains lean concepts seamlessly throughout all operational and functional areas.

Leveling: Evenly distributing over a shift or a day the work required to fulfill customer demand. Leveling is achieved either through implementing *visible pitch* or *heijunka* (load leveling).

Line balancing: A process in which work elements are evenly distributed within a value stream to meet takt time.

Location indicator: A visual workplace element that shows where an item belongs. Lines, arrows, labels, and signboards are all examples of location indicators.

Milestones: An activity that has, or should have, a scheduled completion date or time, and that has a major effect on the timing or completion of a project.

Muda: See *waste.*

Pitch: A multiple of takt time that will allow you to create, maintain, and sustain a consistent and practical workflow throughout the value stream. To calculate pitch, multiply the takt time by the number of work units to flow through the system in a manageable way.

Problem solving: A team working together to follow these steps – defining the problem; analyzing possible causes; identifying possible solutions; developing an action plan; evaluating and renewing the action plan; standardizing effective ideas.

Process: A sequence of operations (consisting of people, materials and methods) for the design, creation and delivery of a product or service.

Pull: A system of creation and delivery in which nothing is produced by the upstream supplier until the downstream supplier signals a need. Pull can operate with single units or small batches. It enables work without preset schedules.

Push: Conventional work in which schedules are pushed along based on sales projections and availability of materials. It leads employees to make as many work units as they can as fast as they can, even if the next process is not ready to use the work units, which causes long queue times.

Queue time: The amount of time a work unit will wait before a downstream process is ready to work on it.

Red tag: A label used in a 5S implementation to identify items that are not needed or that are in the wrong place.

Runner: A worker who ensures that pitch is maintained. The runner covers a designated route within the pitch period, picking up work units, folders, or kanban cards, and delivering them to their appropriate places.

Safety resources: A means of meeting customer demand when internal constraints or inefficiencies disrupt process flow.

Set in order: The second activity in the 5S system. It involves identifying the best location for each item that remains in the area, relocating items that do not belong in the area, setting height and size limits, and installing temporary location indicators.

Shine: The third activity in the 5S system. It involves cleaning everything thoroughly, using cleaning as a form of inspection, and coming up with ways to prevent dirt, grime, and other contaminants from accumulating.

Sort: The first activity in the 5S system. It involves sorting through and sorting out items, placing red tags on these items, and moving them to a temporary holding area. The items are disposed of, sold, moved, or given away by a predetermined time.

Standardize (for 5S): The fourth activity in the 5S system. It involves creating the rules for maintaining and controlling the conditions established after implementing the first three S's. Visual controls are used to make these conditions obvious.

Standardized work: An agreed-upon set of work procedures that establishes the best method and sequence for each process. Standardized work is implemented to maximize efficiency while simultaneously ensuring safe conditions.

Storyboard: A poster-sized framework for holding all the key information for a lean implementation. It contains the outcomes for each of the eight steps of value stream management.

Supermarket: A system used to store a set level of finished-goods inventory or WIP and replenish what is "pulled" to fulfill customer orders (internal and external). A supermarket is used when circumstances make it difficult to sustain continuous flow.

Sustain: The fifth activity of the 5S system, where a person or team ensures adherence to 5S standards through communication, training, and self-discipline.

Takt time: The pace of customer demand. Takt time determines how fast a process needs to run to meet customer demand. Takt time is calculated by dividing the total operating time available by the total quantity required by the customer.

Team charter: A document that includes but that is not limited to the following elements: 1) a clear definition of a team's mission, 2) a statement of team members' roles and responsibilities, 3) a description of the scope of the team's responsibility and authority, 4) project deadlines, 5) a list of metrics and targets, and 6) a list of deliverables (outcomes).

Team leader: The person who facilitates the value stream management process from beginning to end (until a complete kaizen plan is created). The team leader calls and facilitates meetings, ensures that agendas are completed, and manages the allocation and completion of all tasks.

Total cycle time: The total of the cycle times for each individual operation or process or work area in a value stream. Total cycle time ideally equals total value-added time.

Total lead time: The total of all cycle times from all individual processes within the lean office value stream, plus the queue times that exist between each process.

U-shaped cells: A U-shaped, work area layout that allows one or more workers to process and transfer work units one piece—or one small group—at a time.

Value added percentage: The percentage of the total lead time that is spent actually adding value to a work unit. To calculate value added percentage, divide the total cycle time by the total lead time.

Value stream: A collection of all the steps (both value-added and non-value added) involved in making the transformation from raw material to what the customer is willing to pay for.

Value stream champion: The person with the authority and responsibility to allocate the organization's resources during the life of the project. The champion should always be completely committed to the project. It is often the champion who initiates the project.

Value stream management: A sequential, eight-step process used to implement lean concepts and tools derived from the Toyota Production System. The purpose of value stream management is to minimize the waste that prevents a smooth, continuous flow of product throughout the value stream.

Value stream mapping (or value stream process mapping): The visual representation of the material and information flow of a specific product family; Steps 4 and 6 of the value stream management process.

Visible pitch board: A visual control method that will control the flow of work throughout the day, also showing how each person in the value stream receives his or her portion of work.

Waste (also *muda*): Anything within a value stream that adds cost or time without adding value. The seven most common wastes are 1) overproducing, 2) waiting, 3) transport, 4) processing, 5) inventory, 6) motion, and 7) defects and spoilage.

Work unit: A specific, measurable amount of work that can be customized and treated as a whole. Examples of a work unit include an order, a report, or a blueprint.

Work unit family: A group of parts that share common equipment and processing attributes.

Worker balance chart: A visual display of the work elements, times, and workers at each location. It is used to show improvement opportunities by visually displaying the times of each work operation in relation to the total value stream cycle time and takt time.

References

5S and Visual Workplace

Hirano, Hiroyuki. 1995. *5 Pillars of the Visual Workplace: The Sourcebook for 5S Implementation*. New York, NY: Productivity Press.

Peterson, Jim, and Roland Smith. 1998. *5S Pocket Guide*. New York, NY: Productivity Press.

Benchmarking

American Productivity & Quality Center. 1993. *The Benchmarking Management Guide*. New York, NY: Productivity Press.

Camp, Robert C. 1989. *Benchmarking: The Search for Industry Best Practices That Lead to Superior Performance*. New York, NY: Productivity Press.

Damelio, Robert. 1995. *The Basics of Benchmarking*. New York, NY: Productivity Press.

Cell Design

Hyer, Nancy, and Urban Wemmerlöv. 2002. Reorganizing Office Work Using Cellular Principle—Chapter 18 in *Reorganizing the Factory: Competing Through Cellular Manufacturing*. New York, NY: Productivity Press.

Continuous Improvement/Kaizen

Greiner, Donna. 1997. *The Basics of Idea Generation*. New York, NY: Productivity Press.

Imai, Isaki. 1997. *Gemba Kaizen: A Common-Sense Low-Cost Approach to Management*. New York: McGraw-Hill.

Japan Human Relations Association, eds. 1995. *The Improvement Engine: Creativity and Innovation Through Employee Involvement*. New York, NY: Productivity Press.

———. 1997. *Kaizen Teian 1: Developing Systems for Continuous Improvement Through Employee Suggestions*. New York, NY: Productivity Press.

———. 1997. *Kaizen Teian 2: Guiding Continuous Improvement Through Employee Suggestions*. New York, NY: Productivity Press.

Laraia, Anthony C., Patricia E. Moody, and Robert W. Hall. 1999. *The Kaizen Blitz: Accelerating Breakthroughs in Productivity and Performance*. New York: John Wiley & Sons.

Lean/Toyota Production System

Japan Management Association, eds. 1986. *Kanban and Just-In-Time at Toyota: Management Begins at the Workplace*. New York, NY: Productivity Press.

Levinson, William A. 2002. *Henry Ford's Lean Vision: Enduring Principles from the First Ford Motor Plant*. New York, NY: Productivity Press.

Liker, Jeffrey, ed. 1997. *Becoming Lean: Inside Stories of U.S. Manufacturers*. New York, NY: Productivity Press.

Ohno, Taiichi. 1988. *Toyota Production System: Beyond Large-Scale Production*. New York, NY: Productivity Press.

Productivity Press Development Team. 2002. *LeanSpeak: The Productivity Business Improvement Dictionary*. New York, NY: Productivity Press.

Womack, James P. and Daniel T. Jones. 1996. *Lean Thinking: Banish Waste and Create Wealth in Your Corporation*. New York: Simon & Schuster.

Measurement/Assessment

Brown, Mark Graham. 2003. *Baldrige Award Winning Quality: How to Interpret the Baldrige Criteria for Performance Excellence, 12th ed.* New York, NY: Productivity Press.

———. 1996. *Keeping Score: Using the Right Metrics to Drive World-Class Performance*. New York: NY: Productivity Press.

———. 2003. *The Pocket Guide to the Baldrige Award Criteria, 9th ed.* New York, NY: Productivity Press.

———. 2000. *Winning Score: How to Design and Implement Organizational Scorecards*. New York, NY: Productivity Press.

Harbour, Jerry L. 1997. *The Basics of Performance Measurement*. New York, NY: Productivity Press.

Maskell, Brian H. 1996. *Making the Numbers Count: The Management Accountant as Change Agent on the World Class Team*. New York, NY: Productivity Press.

Problem Solving and Process Improvement

Fukuda, Ryuji. 1996. *CEDAC: A Tool for Continuous Systematic Improvement*. New York, NY: Productivity Press.

Kelly, Michael R. 1992. *Everyone's Problem-Solving Handbook: Step-by-Step Solutions for Quality Improvement*. New York, NY: Productivity Press.

Wilson, Ray W. and Paul Harsin. 1998. *Process Mastering: How to Establish and Document the Best Known Way to Do a Job*. New York, NY: Productivity Press.

Process Mapping/Value Stream Mapping

Damelio, Robert. 1996. *The Basics of Process Mapping*. New York, NY: Productivity Press.

Rother, Mike and John Shook. 1999. *Learning to See, Version 1.2*. Brookline, MA: Lean Enterprise Institute, Inc.

Teamwork

Chang, Richard Y. 1999. *Success Through Teamwork: A Practical Guide to Interpersonal Team Dynamics*. San Francisco: Jossey-Bass/Pfeiffer.

Katzenbach, Jon R. and Douglas K. Smith. 1994. *The Wisdom of Teams: Creating the High-Performance Organization*. New York, NY: HarperBusiness.

Lindborg, Henry J. 1997. *The Basics of Cross-Functional Teams*. New York, NY: Productivity Press.

Maurer, Rick. 1994. *Feedback Toolkit: 16 Tools for Better Communication in the Workplace*. New York, NY: Productivity Press.

Michalski, Walter J. 1998. *40 Tools for Cross-Functional Teams: Building Synergy for Breakthrough Creativity*. New York, NY: Productivity Press.

Scholtes, Peter R., Brian Joiner, and Barbara J. Streibel. 1996. *The Team Handbook, 2nd ed.* Madison, WI: Joiner.

Index